W9-BLZ-013

Steinbeck's Literary Dimension:
A Guide to Comparative Studies

edited by

TETSUMARO HAYASHI
Ball State University

The Scarecrow Press, Inc.
Metuchen, N.J.   1973

Library of Congress Cataloging in Publication Data

Hayashi, Tetsumaro, comp.
  Steinbeck's literary dimension.

    CONTENTS: Chronology of John Steinbeck (1902-1968)
--Steele, J. Steinbeck and Charles Dickens.--Ditsky,
J. Steinbeck and William Faulkner. [etc.]
    1. Steinbeck, John, 1902-1968. I. Title.
PS3537.T3234Z714   813'.5'2   72-7457
ISBN 0-8108-0550-2

Dedicated to

BALL STATE UNIVERSITY (Indiana)

and

KENT STATE UNIVERSITY (Ohio)

CONTENTS

PREFACE

The original idea for the comparative essays on John Steinbeck contained in this volume goes back to an article by Professor Peter Lisca (author of The Wide World of John Steinbeck, 1958) entitled "Steinbeck and Hemingway: Suggestions for a Comparative Study." It was written for the memorial number of the Steinbeck Quarterly in the spring of 1968. This study was so well received that shortly after its first appearance it was reprinted in the Span, a USIS-sponsored English-language journal, published in India with a circulation of over 100,000 copies.

Encouraged by the success of this first comparative study, I have since then obtained a carefully selected number of articles in which each respective author juxtaposes Steinbeck with another important literary figure. There is no doubt that these essays comparing and contrasting Steinbeck with other prominent writers, including Milton, Dickens, Faulkner, Hemingway, and others, will be regarded as rather controversial. However, I hope that the book will also prove to be an enlightening one and provide Steinbeck scholars and teachers with suggestions for further comparative studies. Without giving definitive or dogmatic answers, this series might lead to a re-assessment of Steinbeck's often misunderstood artistic achievements.

The bibliographical editor and library co-ordinator of the Steinbeck Quarterly, Donald L. Siefker, has provided the functional and valuable index for this book.

I wish to express my sincere gratitude to the various authors for their dedicated cooperation in this project as well as to Mr. Siefker and my secretaries, Miss Joey Nelson and Miss Joanne Reed.

The following articles were originally published in the Steinbeck Quarterly under my editorship: those of Professors Richard Astro (3, Winter 1970), John Gribben (5, Spring 1972), Lawrence W. Jones (4, Fall 1971), Sanford E. Marovitz (3, Summer 1970), Andreas K. Poulakidas (3, Summer 1970), George

H. Spies, III (4, Spring 1971), and Joan Steele (5, Winter 1972). The article by Professor John Ditsky was originally published in Steinbeck: The Man and His Work, edited by Richard Astro and Tetsumaro Hayashi (Oregon State University Press, 1971) and here revised and enlarged. It was published with the permission of Oregon State University Press and the two editors of the book. Professor Peter Lisca's first article herein is based on his previous article, "Steinbeck and Hemingway," originally published in the Steinbeck Quarterly. Again it was revised and enlarged here. My article on "Steinbeck Scholarship" was based on a previously published article in my John Steinbeck: A Guide to the Doctoral Dissertations (Ball State University, 1971), but revised and enlarged here.

Professor Richard Peterson's article on "Steinbeck and D. H. Lawrence," Professor Warren French's "Steinbeck and J. D. Salinger," and Professor Peter Lisca's second article, "A Survey of Steinbeck Criticism" have never been published before to my knowledge.

The quotations from the works of John Steinbeck used to illustrate the text are reprinted by permission of The Viking Press, Inc., and McIntosh and Otis, Inc., to both of which I am grateful.

Tetsumaro Hayashi
Muncie, Indiana
March, 1972

CHRONOLOGY OF JOHN STEINBECK (1902-1968)*

1902   John Ernst Steinbeck born February 27 in Salinas, California.

1919   Graduated from Salinas High School.

1920   Began intermittent attendance at Stanford University.

1924   First publication, "Fingers of Cloud" and "Adventures in Arcademy," in The Stanford Spectator (February and June).

1925   Left Stanford permanently without a degree. Went to New York City and worked as construction laborer and reporter of The American (newspaper).

1926   Returned to California. Humorous verses published in Stanford Lit: 1. "If Eddie Guest Had Written the Book of Job: Happy Birthday," 2. "If John A. Weaver Had Written Keats' Sonnet in the American Language: On Looking at a New Book by Harold Bell Wright," 3. "Atropos: Study of a Very Feminine Obituary Editor."

1929   Cup of Gold published.

1930   Married Carol Henning and began residence in Pacific Grove. First met Edward F. Ricketts.

1932   Moved to Los Angeles in summer. The Pastures of Heaven published.

1933   Returned to Pacific Grove early in year. To a God Unknown published. Two stories, the first

---

*Note: "LV," passim, refers to The Long Valley, New York: Viking Press, 1938.

9

two parts of The Red Pony ("The Gift" and "The
Great Mountains") published in North American
Review in November and December (later included
in LV).

1934   Olive Hamilton Steinbeck, John's mother, died
        in February. "The Murder" selected as an O.
        Henry prize story and published in O. Henry
        Prize Stories. "The Raid" published in North
        American Review (both in LV).

1935   Tortilla Flat published, bringing immediate fame
        and financial success. Won the Commonwealth
        Club of California Gold Medal, cited as "the
        Year's Best by a Californian." Verses "Mammy,"
        "Baubles," "To a Carmel," "The Visitor," "Four
        Shades of Navy Blue," "The Genius," "Ivanhoe,"
        and "Thoughts on Seeing a Stevedore" published
        in Monterey Beacon. "The White Quail" published
        in North American Review (later in LV). "The
        Snake" published in Monterey Beacon (LV).

1936   In Dubious Battle (California Novel of 1936
        Prize) and "Saint Katy the Virgin" published.
        Moved to Los Gatos, California. His father,
        John Ernst Steinbeck, died in May. Article,
        "The Harvest Gypsies," published in San Fran-
        cisco News in October. Trip to Mexico.

1937   Of Mice and Men published in February. Went
        to New York and Pennsylvania to work on stage
        version, which was produced at Music Box
        Theatre in New York in November and won Drama
        Critics' Circle Silver Plaque for that season. He
        was chosen one of the ten outstanding young men
        of the year. The Red Pony published in three
        parts. First trip to Europe. Later in year,
        went to West from Oklahoma with migrants.
        "The Promise" and "The Ears of Johnny Bear"
        published in Esquire (September 3) (later in
        LV). "The Chrysanthemums" published in
        Harper's Magazine (October 1937).

1938   The Long Valley [LV] and "Their Blood Is
        Strong," pamphlet reprint of "The Harvest
        Gypsies" published. "The Harness" published in
        Atlantic Monthly (LV).

1939   The Grapes of Wrath published.   National Insti-
            tute of Arts and Letters membership given.

1940   The Grapes of Wrath won (1) Pulitzer Prize,
            (2) American Booksellers Association Award,
            and (3) Social Work Today Award.   With Edward
            F. Ricketts, went to Gulf of California on "West-
            ern Flyer" to collect marine invertebrates,
            March-April.   Filmed The Forgotten Village in
            Mexico (the book published in 1941).   The Grapes
            of Wrath (1939) filmed.   Of Mice and Men (1937)
            filmed.

1941   The Forgotten Village published.   "How Edith Mc-
            Gillicuddy Met Robert Louis Stevenson" published
            in Harper's Magazine (later in Portable Stein-
            beck).

1942   Separation and interlocutory divorce from Carol
            Henning.   The Moon Is Down (novel and play)
            published.   Bombs Away written for Army Air
            Corps.   Tortilla Flat filmed.

1943   Married Gwyndolen Conger in March and began
            residence in New York.   Spent several months
            in European war zone as correspondent for New
            York Herald Tribune.   The Moon Is Down filmed
            and also published as a play.   Lifeboat filmed.

1944   Son Thomas born.

1945   Cannery Row published.   The Red Pony repub-
            lished with fourth chapter, "The Leader of the
            People."   "The Pearl of the World" appeared in
            Woman's Home Companion magazine in December.
            A Medal for Benny filmed.   Bought home in
            New York.

1946   Won King Haakon (Norway) Liberty Cross for
            The Moon Is Down.   Filmscript, "A Medal for
            Benny" published.   Son John born.

1947   Trip to Russia with Robert Capa, August-Sep-
            tember.   The Wayward Bus published.   The
            Pearl published and filmed.   Norwegian Award
            for The Moon Is Down.   The Wayward Bus se-
            lected as the Book-of-the-Month-Club book.

1948   Elected to American Academy of Letters.
          Divorced from Gwyn Conger. A Russian Journal
          with Robert Capa, an account of his trip to
          Russia, published. Edward F. Ricketts died.
          A short story, "Miracle of Tepayac," published
          in Collier's.

1949   The Red Pony filmed. A short story, "His
          Father" published in Reader's Digest.

1950   Burning Bright (novel) published. Married to
          Elaine Scott in December. Viva Zapata! filmed.

1951   The Log from the Sea of Cortez published, con-
          taining introduction and narrative from Sea of
          Cortez and biography of Edward F. Ricketts.
          Burning Bright (play) published.

1952   East of Eden published. Sent reports to Collier's
          from Europe.

1954   Sweet Thursday published.

1955   Pipe Dream (Richard Rodgers and Oscar Ham-
          merstein II musical comedy based on Sweet
          Thursday) produced. Editorials for Saturday
          Review. East of Eden (1952) filmed.

1956   The O. Henry Award for "Affair at 7, Rue de
          M. ...."

1957   The Short Reign of Pippin IV published. The
          Wayward Bus (1947) filmed.

1958   Once There Was a War, a collection of wartime
          dispatches, published.

1961   The Winter of Our Discontent published. Book-
          of-the-Month Club Selected The Winter of Our
          Discontent. "Flight" (a short story) filmed in
          San Francisco and independently produced.

1962   Travels with Charley published. Received Nobel
          Prize for Literature in December.

1964   John F. Kennedy Memorial Library Trusteeship
          given. Won Press Medal of Freedom and United
          States Medal of Freedom.

1966   America and Americans published. The John
         Steinbeck Society of America was founded at
         Kent State University by Tetsumaro Hayashi and
         Preston Beyer.

1968   The Steinbeck Quarterly began publication (origi-
         nally entitled, Steinbeck Newsletter).

1969   The Journal of a Novel posthumously published.
         Steinbeck Conference held at the University of
         Connecticut.

1970   Steinbeck Conference held at Oregon State Uni-
         versity.

1971   Steinbeck Monograph Series began publication at
         Ball State University. Steinbeck Conference and
         Film Festival held at San Jose State College in
         February.

Part I

COMPARATIVE ESSAYS

1.   STEINBECK AND CHARLES DICKENS

A Century of Idiots: Barnaby Rudge and Of Mice and Men
by Joan Steele

> His work is a vast, fascinating, paradoxical uni-
> verse ... a celebration of goodness and innocence;
> a display of chaos, violence, corruption and deca-
> dence. It is no neatly shaped and carefully-cul-
> tivated garden of artistic perfections, but a sprawl-
> ing continent of discordant extremes: warmth,
> tenderness and subtlety, but also tastelessness,
> crudity, and sentimentality; brilliant comedy mixed
> with adolescent facetiousness; intense human charity
> and magnanimity fading off into lax and shallow
> morality; powerful vision beside superficial and
> pretentious preaching. [1]

These words of the English critic F. W. Watt appraise
the work of John Steinbeck.   Taken out of context they seem
equally apt to describe that of Charles Dickens.   A century
is not a barrier between two artists who share similar world
views.   In his review of Sweet Thursday entitled "A Narrow-
gauge Dickens," Hugh Holman draws an explicit analogy between the two authors.   He states that Steinbeck "shares
with Charles Dickens the failure to subject his people [either
with or without the external pressures of society] to an
organized and logically consistent philosophy. "[2]   This echoes
George Santayana's opinion that Dickens

> had no ideas on any subject; what he had was a
> vast sympathetic participation in the daily life of
> mankind; and what he saw of ancient institutions
> made him hate them, as needless sources of op-
> pression, misery, selfishness and rancour. [3]

One way to circumvent the problem of philosophical incon-
sistency is to deny the validity of all systems.   Steinbeck
did this in Sea of Cortez when he defined his concept of
"non-teleological thinking" as that which

considers events as outgrowths and expressions
rather than as results ... not with what could be,
or should be, or might be, but rather with what
actually 'is'--attempting at most to answer the already sufficiently difficult questions what or how
instead of why. 4

   If Dickens and Steinbeck are similar in their lack of
systematic philosophy, they also share many other more
positive characteristics noted by Hugh Holman: a tender
spirit, sensitivity to suffering, and forgiveness of weakness
and failure--as well as fascination for, and great success
with the portrayal of eccentrics, grotesques, idiots, children,
and childlike states of mind (p. 20). One of the most provocative parallels in the work of these two men is their use
of idiot and non-rational characters. A comparison of
Barnaby Rudge and Of Mice and Men shows how, through the
portrayal of an idiot's relationship to society, the characters
of Barnaby and Lennie reveal their authors' social attitudes.

   From the title character's first appearance in the
third chapter of Barnaby Rudge he moves through the book
haphazardly, juxtaposed with both "normal" and "abnormal"
characters. Most of these people attempt to manipulate him
in some way, either directly like his companion Hugh, or
indirectly like Lord George Gordon, the leader of the Protes-
tant "Gordon Riots" which comprise much of the action of
the novel. Barnaby's relations with his mother, Mr. Hare-
dale, and Gabriel Varden permit Dickens to comment on his
mental condition through the eyes of respected members of
the community. But Barnaby is also surrounded by foils who
represent in complex ways other facets of sub-rational or
irrational humanity. Symbolically, Gordon, Gashford, Dennis, Sim, Hugh, and even Sir John Chester are representa-
tives of various types of derangement. In his perceptive
study of the novel Harold F. Folland directs attention to the
prevalence of the word "mad" and its synonyms, as well as
to the wide range of irrationality displayed by the riot
leaders, who include

   Gordon, a deluded visionary, Barnaby, a harmless
   imbecile with a vivid imagination, Hugh, a mag-
   nificently powerful animal whose rudimentary reason is undeveloped and untrained, and Dennis, [a]
   hangman with a pathologically sadistic love for his
   job, whose reason is narrow and perverted. 5

Yet these allegorical leaders are not as crazy as the
true leader, Sir John Chester--an instance of the deception
possible when appearance and reality are confused. For the
real villain in Barnaby Rudge is Sir John, who--even if he
is not a lampoon of Lord Chesterfield--is certainly symbolic
of the irresponsibility of the upper classes. On the political
level Sir John is the prime manipulator and evil genius behind the riots. He also functions as one of five irresponsible fathers in the novel whose social role may represent
the political irresponsibility displayed by the upper classes
of the time--another kind of group madness. Dickens' madmen are saved from caricature because they function in
established social roles; the nature of the leadership is itself a commentary by Dickens on the nature of these destructive riots, which run rampant over individual rights.
Barnaby and Gordon represent lesser evils because their
flaw is one of omission rather than commission, although
their gullibility makes them serve Chester's evil ends.

Dickens places Barnaby as an individual character on
a broad and complex canvas. Yet as a symbolic character
rather than a convincing protagonist, Barnaby is really
tangential to the action. In contrast, Of Mice and Men depends upon the relationship between Lennie and George; it
is society's treatment of them which is symbolic. In Steinbeck we are dealing with symbolic action, in Dickens with
symbolic characterization. In Barnaby Rudge the characters
play their roles in the riot because of their character traits;
indeed they are riot participants because of their mentalities.
In Of Mice and Men the focus is on society's role in relation to the protagonists. Both novels, however, succeed in
reflecting the disparate problems of their societies.

We see this even in such a matter as title. Dickens
uses the name of an individual--an "idiot"--for the title of
his novel, yet the action transcends the fate of Barnaby or
of any one character and presents a view of social relationships beyond the limits of time and place. Steinbeck chooses
a title with a broad scope, one which is meant to imply the
universality of the novel's message, but the action is focused
on the microcosm of two seemingly unimportant members of
contemporary society. We see clearly in Of Mice and Men
the dilemma of human relationships that Steinbeck perfects
and amplifies in The Grapes of Wrath.

Critics and literary psychologists have studied the
mental aberrations of both Barnaby and Lennie to gain in-

sight into their authors' rationales. Both Barnaby and Lennie are idiots insofar as they exist outside of time. They
have little conception of the passage of time. Barnaby
thinks it must be his birthday when his mother appears to
be upset and distraught, since this is her usual manner on
that day which recalls such unpleasant memories. But his
birthday had passed just a few short weeks before. Lennie
cannot remember the events that took place in Weed when
they were run out of town after he fondled the girl's dress.
Barnaby can picture a life of peace and happiness resulting
from the violence of mob action only because he is incapable of understanding reality. Barnaby's importance makes
some analysis of his mental state crucial to an understanding of his symbolic function, although it is not necessary to
go so far as L. M. H. Brush's "case history" in which she
analyzes him as a "clear case of a regression psychosis of
the paraphrenic type, wholly psychogenic in origin."[6] When
Barnaby first appears, Dickens uses dialogue skillfully to
convey the quality of the idiot's derangement. Barnaby and
Gabriel Varden have discovered a mysterious wounded man:

> 'Hush!' said Barnaby, laying his fingers upon his
> lips. 'He went out to-day a-wooing. I wouldn't
> for a light guinea that he should never go a-wooing
> again, for, if he did, some eyes would grow dim
> that are not as bright as--see, when I talk of
> eyes, the stars come out! Whose eyes are they?
> If they are angels' eyes, why do they look down
> here and see good men hurt, and only wink and
> sparkle all the night?' ....
>
> 'I can't touch him!' cried the idiot falling back,
> and shuddering as with a strong spasm; 'he's
> bloody!'[7]

The disjointed speech with its symbolic mention of the stars
serving as eyes to differentiate appearance from reality turns
swiftly to the monomania of Barnaby's blood-fixation. Thus
two essential elements of his character are established
through both the tone and content of his speech.

     Barnaby and Lennie are both intimately involved with
animals, and both have unusual dreams that are important
manifestations of their symbolic roles. Barnaby is an idiot
who exists at the level of childhood and only briefly rises
from that level. Abandoned by a villainous father, his devotion to his mother is intense. He is close to nature and

animals, especially to the brutish Hugh of Maypole and to
his pet raven, Grip, who functions actively in the story.
That Dickens foresaw a purposive relationship between Barnaby and his pet is evident in his letter of 28 January 1841
to George Cattermole: "Barnaby being an idiot, my notion
is to have him always in company with a pet raven, who is
immeasurably more knowing than himself. "[8] The raven
voices Dickens' negative view of rebellion through his constant repetition of "I'm a devil, " and Dickens calls him "the
embodied spirit of evil" in Chapter XXV (p. 192). Grip also barks like a dog, which links him to the animality of
Hugh and foreshadows Barnaby's sheltering of Hugh's dog
after his friend's execution.

Barnaby's relationship with Hugh is more complex.
Hugh lures him into joining the mob, and continues to lead
him throughout the riots. Dickens makes his condition quite
clear. Hugh resembles Barnaby, but Hugh is so grotesque
that, according to Folland, he is "dehumanized and unable
to use his strength rationally in his own behalf" (p. 410).
Barnaby's moral superiority is evident from Hugh's admis-
sion that Barnaby's prayers suffice for them both.

The interrelated roles of these three characters are
important. Although Grip speaks of himself as being evil,
he does nothing evil--indeed he is offered no alternatives.
Hugh constantly makes choices for evil, while Barnaby does
not choose--he is good. All three are involved in a social
action which Dickens deplores, but only the activist pays the
penalty.

Steinbeck's use of animals is different. They are
symbolic, passive stage props that increase the depth of the
action. The mouse that Lennie fondles and kills is merely
the precursor of the puppy that meets the same end. The
puppy in turn foreshadows the fate of Curley's wife. Perhaps Steinbeck was thinking of the slang "mouse" to refer
to a woman. Certainly Curley's wife is repeatedly called a
"rat trap" and a "bitch, " although she really deserves her
fate no more than the helpless puppy. The mouse's fate is
that of all men, Steinbeck seems to be saying, and insofar
as this is true he changes Burns's meaning, for Burns's
quotation implies that plans may go wrong, while the action
of Of Mice and Men indicates that such plans will go wrong.

Barnaby's plans appear in dreams of gold reflected
in the gleam of the rural sunset as "that gold which is

piled up yonder in the sky" (p. 342). The gold is an end in
itself: "a rare thing, and say what you will, a thing you
would like to have, I know," as he says to his mother (p.
361). But this gold is suffused in the vague haze of wish-
fulfillment reflected by the metaphoric connection of wealth
to nature's beauty. Significantly, it is to the peace of rural
seclusion that Barnaby will retire at the end of the book.
He had dreamed of an urban glory through participation in
the storming of the London bastions, but his future is to be
rural, for Dickens states in his conclusion that Barnaby
could not be persuaded to return to the city. We almost
envy Barnaby both his escape and his idiocy. Dickens'
negative view of group social action, subject to delusion
and manipulation by irresponsible leaders, is reinforced
by the double image of escape from reality implied in
Barnaby's idiocy and his retreat to a rural idyll.

        In contrast to Barnaby's dreams of gold and urban
glory, Lennie dreams of a practical rural life, detailed even
to the descriptions of its daily chores. He and George as-
pire to a small piece of land that will make them part of a
stable and secure society instead of its migratory fringes.
George ritually repeats, "we'd belong there ... we'd know
what comes of our planting."[9] Lennie and George's dream
is more than materialistic; it envisions a place where "nobody gonna hurt nobody nor steal from 'em" (p. 116). In
fact, as the Negro, Crooks, sees only too clearly, it is
"just like heaven.... Nobody ever gets to heaven, and nobody gets no land" (p. 81). Yet George and Lennie's piece
of land has a specific setting in time and place, and they believe they can achieve their dream through real means.

        Barnaby is better off for not achieving his goal, as
Dickens makes clear by his linking of blood and gold in Mrs.
Rudge's speech: "Do you not see," she said, "how red it
is? Nothing bears so many stains of blood, as gold" (p.
342). But Barnaby as an idiot never thinks beyond the abstract image of the glittering gold and would not have known
what to do with it if his dream became reality. Lennie and
George's defeat is much more humanly tragic in its effect,
for their dream could have come true and together they
could have made it work.

        In addition to dreams of the future, both idiots have
hallucinatory visions that reveal a great deal about them.
As Brush observes, Barnaby's narrative dreams contain
faces that are "images of the daytime people with their

sneers, grins, and teasings" (p. 29). But he also has symbolic dream-nightmares marked by specters and a gothic
horror of blood: "Is it in the room as I have seen it in my
dreams, dashing the ceiling and the walls with red?" he
asks his mother hysterically (p. 133). Although Dickens'
conception of Barnaby's dreams is psychologically valid, he
uses it more superficially than Steinbeck. Given Barnaby's
history, he would fear both ridicule and blood; his hallucina-
tions do not function to explain deep character or action as
Lennie's final visions do.

Lennie also has two kinds of dreams. His narrative
dream is of a reality from the past--Aunt Clara and her
frighteningly true analysis of his future plight, phrased in
emphatic language:

> And then from out of Lennie's head there came a
> little fat old woman. She wore thick bull's-eye
> glasses and she wore a huge gingham apron with
> pockets, and she was starched and clean....
> 'You're always sayin' that ["I won't be no more
> trouble to George"] an' you know sonafabitching
> well you ain't never gonna do it' [pp. 110-111].

But Lennie's symbolic hallucination is most important. Like
Barnaby's blood fear, Lennie's fixation arises from the far-
thest depths of his mind in the form of a gigantic rabbit.
This is doubly a dream rabbit, for it is the symbol of the
utopian farm, made monstrous in size and cruel in speech.
It sneers and grins at Lennie, and teases him, while, because it speaks in his own voice, it makes Lennie himself
appear to be dream-like and visionary. The dream-rabbit's
berating of Lennie prepares the reader for the catastrophe,
for when one's most cherished dream turns upon one, it is
indeed the death of hope.

Lennie's animals, real and imaginary, are better foils
for him as a skillfully characterized idiot than are Barnaby's.
Lennie does not have an understanding of his relationship to
these animals as Barnaby seems to have with Grip. The
idea of the talking raven as an idiot's foil is also a bit too
pat for the modern reader to accept; one would prefer to
think of the idiot as having at least the same level of intelligence as the animals that function symbolically.

Dickens, as we have seen, oversimplifies Barnaby in
a world beyond his understanding so that we almost envy him.

This idealization of instinctive good by placing it upon an
idiot is a kind of anti-intellectual sentimentality which causes
the theme of the novel to flounder.   Modern critics have
charged Steinbeck with similar sentimentalism and anti-intel-
lectualism.   Frederick J. Hoffman objects to Steinbeck's re-
duction of man to the animal level, noting that

> the idiots of Steinbeck's fiction are a case in point;
> there is no attempt to make us realize their idiocy
> in the perspective of a larger fictional strategy;
> instead we are reduced to a comparable sub-ration-
> al level of appreciation and sympathy. [10]

Yet it is most important to see Steinbeck's treatment as highly metaphoric.   All men are animals; when one of them fails
to transcend this animal level in his social relationships it
is a cause for sorrow to the whole human race.   Thus, the
only real obligation an author has is to make his character
believable--to make, in this case, the delineation of an abnormal state of mind so plausible as to cause the reader to
accept the fiction wholly.   Once the reader has entered into
the sphere of belief, has established a rapport with the
character, idiot or not, then he will be able to see the
"larger fictional strategy" which involves, in Lennie's case,
the symbolic use of the abnormal personality toward a specific end.   Steinbeck had a particular goal in mind with
Lennie.   He "was to be, not a pathetic cretin, but a symbolic figure with earth longings, a Lennie who was not to
represent insanity at all, but the inarticulate and powerful
yearnings of all men. "[11]

     In contrast to Barnaby's relations with a large num-
ber of characters, George is the pivot around which Lennie
revolves.   Of Mice and Men's believability results from
their reciprocal relationship.   Although George is a father-
figure to Lennie and has the position of authority, he often
complains that if it were not for Lennie he could be free to
sojourn in "cat houses" and drink quantities of rotgut booze.
Yet George does not really want this kind of freedom.   He
prefers the dream that he and Lennie share, and he would
never attain that dream without Lennie.   Paradoxically, he
cannot attain the dream with Lennie either, for Lennie's
mentality makes the conscious striving for any goal impossible.   But Lennie keeps the dream alive for George.   He
tells Candy that Lennie "usta like to hear about it so much
I got to thinking maybe we would" (p. 103).   George is not
a pathetic character, as many critics have contended, for,

as Warren French notes, he has "a will and he exercises it
to make two critical decisions at the end of the novel--to
kill Lennie and to lie about it. "12 He is really killing that
aspect of himself that Lennie represents. When he goes off
with Slim, abandoning the possibility of joining with Candy
and his nest-egg, Steinbeck indicates that it is only the mentally muddled who ever believe in the fulfillment of dreams--
the rational mind sees the truth of Burns's quotation.

In Of Mice and Men there are only ten characters,
but each can be read as a kind of synecdoche for his social
group. George as Lennie's surrogate father does not evade
his responsibility. Moreover, George's role is both pater-
nal and fraternal; the brotherhood that exists between these
two makes their harsh life bearable for both. As George
puts it: "We got somebody to talk to that gives a damn
about us" (p. 15). The characters that move about this
pair are strongly linked to the themes of the novel. The
Boss is a peripheral figure--one of strong but remote authority, and freedom of action. (Only he and Slim have
been in Crooks's room.) The Boss represents the nonlabor-
ing man; he wears high-heeled boots and spurs to distinguish
him from his workmen. But his authority is too remote and
borders on irresponsibility as we see through the actions of
his son Curley, a wild and vicious troublemaker who cannot
control either his own life or his wife. Slim, the head
mule-skinner, on the other hand, represents the proper use
of authority: "His word was taken on any subject, be it
politics or love" (p. 37). It is significant that Slim is apparently of the same social class as Lennie and George; he
transcended their limitations and has thereby become a kind
of liaison between the groups.

Crucial to the development of theme is Crooks. He
represents both a group and a condition; he is a Negro and
he is maimed. We learn that Crooks once had the kind of
earth attachment--"the little chicken ranch" of his childhood
--that Lennie and George want. It did not work then for
him because of his color, and he withdraws from participation in the present dream when he is degraded by his cultural enemy, white womanhood.

Another maimed grotesque is Candy, the "swamper, "
whose defects are his age and his loss of a hand. Candy
wants to invest his $300 in the dream, but Steinbeck suggests
that he is unworthy because he will not, or cannot, accept
responsibility. Where George forces himself to shoot Lennie

to keep him from suffering, Candy cannot bring himself to
shoot his suffering old dog and lets Carlson do it for him.
To reinforce the analogy, Candy reacts to the death of the
dog and the death of Lennie in nearly the same way: "He
rolled slowly over and faced the wall and lay silent" (p. 54)
on hearing Carlson's shot; "Old Candy lay down in the hay
and covered his eyes with his arm" (p. 108) as the men go
out after Lennie.

Because George has been able to live up to his re-
sponsibilities, he dispatches Lennie to his only hope of "that
place"--through death, and then throws the gun on the ashes
of their old campfire--the ashes of a dream. It is Slim who
understands George's state of mind at this moment. They
go off together to the town, away from the blasted and with-
ered dream by the banks of the peaceful river.

This discussion of similar elements in Dickens and
Steinbeck opened with a criticism of Steinbeck that seemed
equally valid for Dickens. The likeness is reinforced by
George Orwell's comments on Dickens:

> His radicalism is of the vaguest kind and yet one
> always knows that it is there. That is the differ-
> ence between being a moralist and a politician.
> He has no constructive suggestions, not even a
> clear grasp of the society he is attacking, only
> an emotional perception that something is wrong. [13]

Steinbeck, like Dickens, promotes reform rather than revolution. Although his work is full of violence he does not per-
suade to violence but rather to amelioration through human
understanding. Steinbeck, despite his whores and vulgarity,
is a moralist because he uses the novelist's tools to describe elements of his society that cry out for change, and
because his is essentially a moral view that seeks what Peter
Lisca calls "adjustment through mutual understanding and acceptance."[14] At the same time Lisca is quite correct in
denying that Of Mice and Men is a "glorification of idiocy"
(p. 15). Beneath the deceptively smooth surface of the novel lie turbulent forces. Lennie's catastrophe results more
from his irresponsibility and violence than from his idiocy.
Lennie's utopia has to be destroyed because he is a "loner"
whose madness precludes his cooperating with George and
hence working constructively toward their mutual goal. Steinbeck tells us that mass society is an evil, against which the
individual has no chance unless he unites with others to

achieve his goals.   Irresponsible individualism brings death
and destruction.

Dickens enlisted the Gordon Riots of a hundred years
earlier in his plea for a better understanding of the problems of his own times, and chose several irrational characters to present the negative as an inducement toward the
positive.   Barnaby can survive because he is the most pas-
sively innocent element from the irrational "complex."
Barnaby does not get the kind of utopia he dreams of, but
he gets a substitute that is nearer to the dream than he realizes.
Once removed from a milieu he never comprehends, he attains
a kind of peaceful individual seclusion that in its way is quite
relevant to Dickens' conception of the value of the individual.

Given these two works and the significant differences
a close analysis reveals, why should John Steinbeck in the
twentieth century be considered a "narrow-gauge Dickens"?
Both men were products of the middle class from which they
rose to positions of eminence transcending class boundaries.
Early in their careers both shared an unconcern for abstract
philosophical systems along with a deep concern for society
and its members. 15   The result was that both built their social themes on character and delineated unique characters
whose world is personal and microcosmic.   "Dickensian" is
a convenient cliché that embraces "originals" like Mr. Dick,
Mr. Micawber, Jenny Wren, and Miss Havisham, as well as
Fauna, Joseph and Mary Rivas, Hazel, and Grandpa Joad.
Because they develop philosophic patterns that originate in
human relationships, both authors expend their talents on
the detailed characterization and description that create
"originals."   Possibly the early picaresque Dickens and
the late picaresque Steinbeck have reversed their patterns
of growth.   But critics today see much more in Pickwick
than did readers of the nineteenth century.   It would not be
surprising if succeeding generations found more than con-
vivial sentimentality in Steinbeck's later work.

<h3 style="text-align:center">Notes</h3>

1. F. W. Watt, Steinbeck (Edinburgh: Oliver and Boyd,
       1962), p. 2.

2. New Republic, 130 (7 June 1954), 18-20.

3. "Dickens, " in The Dickens Critics, ed. George H. Ford

and Lauriat Lane, Jr. (Ithaca, N.Y.: Cornell University Press, 1961), p. 137.

4. Quoted in Antonia Seixas, "John Steinbeck and the Non-teleological Bus, " in Steinbeck and His Critics, ed. E. W. Tedlock, Jr. and C. V. Wicker (Albuquerque: University of New Mexico Press, 1957), p. 277. Although Sea of Cortez is a later work, the original title of Of Mice and Men, "Something that Happened," indicates Steinbeck's earlier philosophical attitude.

5. "The Doer and the Deed: Theme and Pattern in Barnaby Rudge, " PMLA, 74 (1959), 409.

6. "A Psychological Study of Barnaby Rudge, " Dickensian, 31 (1935), 29.

7. Charles Dickens, Barnaby Rudge (1841; reprint, London: Oxford University Press, 1954), pp. 28-29. All future quotations will be taken from this edition.

8. Walter Dexter, ed., The Letters of Charles Dickens (Bloomsbury: Nonesuch, 1938), I, 297.

9. John Steinbeck, Of Mice and Men (1937; reprint, New York: Bantam, 1955), p. 63. All future quotations will be taken from this edition.

10. The Modern Novel in America (New York: Gateway, 1956), p. 164.

11. Steinbeck, quoted in Watt, pp. 61-62.

12. John Steinbeck (New York: Twayne, 1961), p. 74.

13. "Charles Dickens, " in Ford and Lane, p. 168.

14. The Wide World of John Steinbeck (New Brunswick, N.J.: Rutgers University Press, 1958), p. 203.

15. An interesting parallel exists in the canons. Barnaby Rudge was Dickens' fifth novel; Of Mice and Men was Steinbeck's sixth novel.

2.   STEINBECK AND WILLIAM FAULKNER

Faulkner and Steinbeck: Men and the Land
by John Ditsky

Surely the names of John Steinbeck and William Faulkner would be among the first--if not in fact the first--to
spring to the mind of anyone contemplating a study of the
relevance of Nature to character in the fiction of twentieth-
century Americans.[1] Yet, though numerous parallels exist,
there are outstanding differences between the two men, not
merely in the ways in which they exploit a common theme,
but in the substance and style of their public careers.   I
suggest that the relatively constant employment of a regu-
larly organized set of attitudes towards Nature, especially
as a force in fiction, distinguishes Faulkner's writing from
that of Steinbeck, whose use of such elements is subject to
variation that indicates a far-from-settled point of view towards their value.

I

John Steinbeck and William Faulkner were both elected to the National Institute of Arts and Letters on January
18, 1939, and the coincidence is itself typical of the quality
of the interrelationship of the two men during the course of
their careers.   In effect, Faulkner and Steinbeck (both at
the mid-point of their creative lives) were being linked together from without--by their readership--in a way neither
man might have expected.

There is, in fact, little public acknowledgement by
either man of the other's work, or his existence.   Beyond
a shared interest in journalism (as with Hemingway), flir-
tations with Hollywood and the stage, and a fascination for
the behavior of men under the stresses of wartime, there
are few evident parallels in their careers that might give us
the comfort of having an objective (if mechanical) basis for
comparison.   In terms of critical favor, Steinbeck was clear-

28

ly falling while Faulkner (after 1945-1946 and the Cowley
Portable Faulkner, but especially after the 1950 reception
of the Nobel Prize) rose to great heights. But we do have
a real subjective basis for such a comparison in what critical usage and reader habit have long since established:
similarities in theme and subject that far outweigh in importance the lucky meeting or the chance comment. Steinbeck would probably agree that there is an essential wisdom
in readers who insist upon the sort of arbitrary but demon-
strably valid pairing that the National Institute of Arts and
Letters election implies.

   Both men were so much the partial victims of their
own mistaken public images--Faulkner as southern decadent,
Steinbeck as spokesman for the proletariat--that their common interests could not at once appear. Indeed, Faulkner's
consistent criticism of writers who treat Man as a creature
subject to his "glands, " instead of as a responsible individual
with a potential integrity, would seem at least partly directed
toward the Steinbeck of early reputation. And Steinbeck's
emphasis upon the common man's resilience--and his further
ability to become mobile in a crisis, and then to form together in groups as a stronger, indefatigable Man--seems at
least partly an answer to the Faulknerian glorification of
patient, enduring, and stable individual men who cede no
portion of themselves to others.

   Yet there was an undeniable movement between these
polarities (insofar as they were even true). Steinbeck
learned to adjust the group-man concept away from the
World-War-proved dangers of mob-party governments until,
by the time of East of Eden and The Winter of Our Discontent, he was as much a moralist as a Faulkner could wish
for. 2 And Faulkner, for all his talk about individuals leav-
ening the sorry mass, tended to show the single man as
tragic, doomed, and failed, with only the race surviving,
enduring, and "prevailing. " Faulkner's own career shows
a significant adjustment in his earlier theories, and interestingly ends with the individual triumphs of The Reivers.
In matters of race, for example, Faulkner had to learn that
his consistent nonsense-usage "the Negro" was neither particularly useful nor really legitimate, and that distinct individuals like Lucas Beauchamp could and would emerge
from this heretofore largely undistinguished group. Steinbeck's earlier prejudices--his Orientals, and his patronizing-
ly stereotyped Spanish-Americans in Tortilla Flat--gradually
disappear as the writer matures. 3 In both cases, therefore,

there was an evident coming together in ideological terms,
however unaware the men themselves might have been of the
working of the process.

To return, then to that essentially correct layman's
judgment--that Faulkner and Steinbeck may best be compared
under the aspect of their attitudes towards Nature, or the
land--we might begin by noting the implications of the term
"regionalist" as applied to both men. There are more similarities than differences between Faulkner's Yoknapatawpha /
Lafayette County and Steinbeck's Salinas, and they make the
comparisons to follow scarcely dependent upon particular
region than upon the -ism both men share: the desire to
render life in universal terms through the observation of
special detail. Thus the Mississippi-California polarity is
a good deal less important than what both men achieve in
spite of it: a common attention to the fictional embodiment
of local--but fully "human"--truth that transcends the soil it
is based upon.

What is most surprising to the student of Nature
themes in Faulkner is the discovery that there exists in his
work a career-long devotion to a tightly-organized and con-
sciously-applied personal "code" of beliefs, from which the
single book may sometimes stray, but not the man. One is
able to find the basically agrarian principles of the Nobel
Prize address in his earliest attempts at writing prose, and
one is furthermore able to see that Faulkner's eventual discovery of the right means of turning those principles into
fiction through the exploitation of the man-Nature relationship was a moment of conversion after which he could lapse
into other interests only at the greatest peril to his artistry.
For convenience and clarity, I distinguish five varieties of
the use of Nature themes in Faulkner: 1) land as chronicle
of human activity; 2) as the basis for dynastic establishment;
3) as the symbol for a covenant with man; 4) as a link with
the pagan past and the "dark forces" of fertility, sexuality,
etc.; and 5) as a symbol of "good" and "natural" influences
in human personality.

Instead of the structural analysis to which Faulkner's
work readily lends itself, the novels of John Steinbeck show
no "system, " but a large number of manifestations of what
may be termed a religion of Nature. Repetition of devices
lends his work a certain ritualistic predictability at times,
and even contributes to his evident successes, but it is also
to blame for the frequently exaggerated intimacy between

man and the land that goes beyond theme and symbol, beyond even the pathetic fallacy, into what must be called--if not in the usual sense--sentimentality. Granted, both men were interested at times--to the confusion of their critics--in the revival of such traditional modes of fiction as the fable and the parable, but the fact remains that for Steinbeck the artistic struggle has been one of trying repeatedly, with varying degrees of success, for restraint in the imaginative employment of his often unruly California species of the otherwise universal truths of Nature. This restraint is more often present than has been generally admitted, but its attainment was the battle of Steinbeck's career, and will be the determinant of his final reputation.

II

   At the earliest stage of their careers, differences in approach to Nature were already apparent. Faulkner's novice pieces, written in the cosmopolitan literary milieu of New Orleans, already displayed the five types of Nature-usage I have described--five full years before the collection of essays by Ransom, Tate, Young, and others that became the classic agrarian manifesto of 1930, I'll Take My Stand: The South and the Agrarian Tradition. Quickly deciding that art ought to be "provincial,"4 Faulkner called for a native drama that would present profoundly American themes: the vital interplay between mobile, rational men and a lifegiving, timeless earth (93-97). Thus his own prose sketch "The Hill," the first known piece by Faulkner in which the sense of locale--a type of Yoknapatawpha County setting--is significant, is important as a personal response to his own plea (90-92). Praising the "beauty of being of the soil like a tree" (117), Faulkner was already using the concept of a pact with the land to define men who are good, producers of life, and servants of Nature's purposes--like the Steinbeck to come. For the early Faulkner, the references are Greek and--as a bridge to the symbolist and decadent poets-- Keatsian. Finding "entrails; masculinity" beneath the "spiritual beauty" of the Urn ode (117), Faulkner naturally widened his association of Nature with manhood to include human virtue as well; the young Steinbeck, meanwhile, was writing college humor, and began his career as a novelist without a set of published prior assumptions.

   If the apprenticeship novels of the two men are compared, the distinction becomes increasingly evident. In Cup of Gold (1929), Nature's use is unremarkable: pathetic fal-

lacy, the exotic landscape of Wales, and what Merlin calls
the "green monotony" of the Indies. [5] Henry progresses
from the ideal Elizabeth's "flowering body" (21-24, 27) to
"Mother Jungle" in Panama (124-127) in his search for the
"harsh, dangerous beauty of lightning" of the Red Saint (139-
141), and when disappointed turns his back on Nature and
natural fulfillment (and his "naked and unashamed" dreams
of Elizabeth), but no defined and personal sense of Nature's
literary possibilities is apparent. Only as Henry approaches
peace in the "immeasurable dark grotto" of "Brother Death"
(196-198)--the first appearance of the cave-in-Nature motif--
does Steinbeck make a tentative gesture towards authority
over his materials.

        Faulkner's immature writings are more extensive
than Steinbeck's, and begin with the New Orleans Sketches
of 1925. The literal importance of character attitude towards the land is established in "Sunset, " where a black
man tragically mistakes the Mississippi Delta for the Africa
of his dreams. [6] A character can be as explicitly land-
related as "The Longshoreman, " musing upon Nature as
blood and fire: "... Ah God, the singing blood, the sultry
blood, singing to the fierce fire in the veins of girls, singing the ancient embers into flame!" (9).

        Greek myth and proper sexuality are identified as
functions of the blood-aspect of the land, even to the point
of fatality: death is part of Nature, the Franciscan "little
sister" (86-91) who is sibling to Steinbeck's "Brother Death."
Finally, the pastoral simplicity of David in "Out of Nazareth"
shows Faulkner as interested as Steinbeck in extracting the
essence of Christianity from the supposedly emasculating influence of churches. David eats "frankly, like an animal, "
and carries Housman with him (50); as with Steinbeck, a
natural simplicity is being praised that makes it difficult to
tell sheep from shepherd.

        Faulkner's first two novels show incomplete assimi-
lation of his own prior reasoning into fictional form. Soldiers' Pay (1926) establishes the timelessness achieved by
man in Nature, as in the "Niggers and mules" interlude. [7]
It is "the earth, watching the wheel of the world, the terrible calm, inevitability of life" (244), an existence to which
sex and death are "the front door and the back door" (295).
Mosquitoes (1927) uses its title-insects as negative symbols,
features of a swamp world like the dawn of time where the
Nausikaa cruises. An artist's ideal of feminity, the "vir-

ginal breastless torso of a girl,"[8] is embodied in Patricia
Robyn, "sexless" yet "disturbing," though balanced by the
cowlike Jenny, whose "white troubling placidity" is more
fully human because more "natural" (55, 83). An artistic
statement of the "dark and measured beating of the heart of
things" (330), Mosquitoes praises those who refuse to tram-
mel up their natural inclinations, but who seek instead a
balance between intellectuality and feeling. Characters such
as Januarius Jones and Talliaferro can be seen as incomplete humans in terms of their nature-covenants, while
Faulkner's saints in Nature (cow-women, idiots, madmen)
may be defective as characters but are thematic idealizations
of natural goodness. Still to come are such near-devils of
inhumanity as Jason and Flem, who are insensitive to Nature. In between are those individuals, like Ratliff and
Stevens, who can see and choose, and who try to live a
rational life-with-Nature. Their predicament is the artist's;
the balance they seek is precisely the one sought by Steinbeck as creator: the problem of endowing human materials
with value in an amoral system.

In Sartoris (1929), the quest for order is defined by
the contrast between the vitality of the Sartorises when the
soil had full meaning for them, and their tragic decline and
dissipation in the landless present. Dynastic implications
are actually less important to Faulkner than is often thought;
I distinguish three classes of characters under this Nature-
topic: 1) dynasts, who acquire land so as to establish families upon it (an initial misuse that brings eventual downfall);
2) non-dynasts, whose relationship with the land may be profound, but does not involve possession for progeny's sake,
or even ownership; 3) the anti-dynasts, who are oblivious to
or contemptuous of the land. Without its consistent soil-
referent, dynasty becomes something else for Faulkner and
Steinbeck: group-morality, heredity, social relationships:
any of several topics which may involve blood ties without
land ties. Steinbeck's The Pastures of Heaven (1932) is a
correspondingly ambitious attempt to deal with dynastic issues; just as the valley of the title makes the book into a
novel of sorts, two running narratives of family unify the
whole: that of the Munroes, who have shaken off their own
great curse only to loose "baby curses" upon the valley;
and that of the Whitesides, whose grand and noble dreams
are the social opposite to the Munroes' but are inextricably
connected with them. The chain of marriages and near-
marriages illustrates this linking, as in its embodiment of
the Eden-motif--a major step towards the themes of Stein-

beck's mature works--the land dominates everyone, whether
as "curse" or as "promise. "

But though the theme of dynasty recurs throughout
Steinbeck's later work, consistency in the use of it is lacking, as To a God Unknown (1933) illustrates. Employing the
densest concentration of Nature-imagery in all of Steinbeck's
fiction, To a God Unknown is a double example of Steinbeck's
failure to learn a lesson: the abandonment of a successful
approach to dynastic themes is the cue for an uncontrolled
handling of an unfamiliar one. In its disproportion between
image or symbol and plot and character as formal entities,
this novel's failure evidences Steinbeck's real sentimentality:
not the extension of sympathy to men at odds with their situations, but the excessive reliance upon Nature as force and
presence to the exclusion of other agencies of realistic character motivation. Opening with a consciously Biblical scene, 9
Steinbeck plays upon the name "Valley of Our Lady": meaning not Mary, Mother of God, but Nature, Mother of Man, it
is land with a "curious femaleness" to it. Joseph Wayne
feels that he is going to a "wise and beautiful woman" (3-4);
and after the "throbbing" land acquires more anthropomorphic
qualities, there follows the fantastic rite of sexual possession:

> 'It's mine, ' he chanted. 'Down deep it's mine,
> right to the center of the world. ' He stamped his
> feet into the soft earth. Then the exultance grew
> to be a sharp pain of desire that ran through his
> body in a hot river. He flung himself face down-
> ward on the grass and pressed his cheek against
> the wet stems. His fingers gripped the wet grass
> and tore it out, and gripped again. His thighs beat
> heavily on the earth [7-8].

The revival of pagan religious customs, the father's spirit's
presence in a tree, the feverish desire for "increase"--every-
thing leading up to the scenes at the fertility-altar in the
woods is a consistent excess, an indication of Steinbeck's
groping towards a personal language of Nature that might
work within the limits of the traditional novel. Fascinating
as this work is--right up to its deliberate inversion of the
Christian tree of bloody sacrifice of a divine Son in Joseph's
act of bringing his son to the father-tree (110-114), followed
eventually by the series of sacrifices that culminates in Joseph's blood-letting and rain-bringing (178-181)--one cannot
get over the sheer heavy-handedness of its approach to Nature.
To a God Unknown is Steinbeck's Mosquitoes.

But Faulkner was already at the stage of The Sound
and the Fury (1929) and As I Lay Dying (1930):   major works
that sustain the developments of the apprentice pieces in all
the categories I have posited.   In the former, Dilsey as
patient and enduring Negro actualizes the land's timelessness; the latter uses such agencies as the river to objectify
the backdrop against which Bundrens plod or scuttle ("It is
as though the space between us were time: an irrevocable
quality"). [10] Quentin's madness is aggravated by the thought
that his family would "swap Benjy's pasture" for him, a
judgment of dynastic misdoing that even Jason confirms when
he admits that "the folks that live on it" have done nothing
for their land. [11]   Though Anse Bundren speaks of the need
for man to "stay put ... like a tree" (34-35), Anse himself
has never heard what Addie calls the land's "voice" in the
blood (165).   God created "sin," says Addie (166), and the
acknowledgement of the sin's naturalness is the acceptance
of Nature.   Quentin's obsession with Caddy is expressed in
land-imagery, as is its counterpart of Darl for Dewey Dell;
both boys find sexuality frightening, even disgusting.   Addie,
Dewey Dell, and Caddy: all are one or another degree of
commitment to the blood's call, and thus are demonstrations
of what Dewey Dell signifies to Darl by her breasts and
thighs: "the horizons and valleys of the earth" and "that
caliper which measures the length and breadth of life" (156,
97-98).   With Addie, we have the intellectualization of the
commitment: words are ways for "dead" men like Anse to
use one another; a word is "just a shape to fill a lack"
(164).   Deeds are all.

At this point, there would be profit in a comparison
of the use of Nature with respect to character through the
rest of Faulkner's major period with what Steinbeck accom-
plishes in his.   The technique of Tortilla Flat (1935) is well
suited to its author's intention.   A mock-epic, it begins with
an ironic Huck Finn disclaimer that leaves the reader con-
sidering just how Danny and his friends might be "gods"
after all.   Such devices as retreats to the woods, the use
of wine to assist communion with and sympathy for the
things of Nature, and a simplicity of character again related to the Nature-loving St. Francis develop the materials
which Steinbeck's healthy irony keeps in check.   In Dubious
Battle (1936) applies these developments to the conventional
novel of social problems.   Much dog-imagery, contrasted as
in Faulkner with war-produced "cattle," and the repeated
use of the cave-in-Nature motif complement Steinbeck's full
control of his materials, and the achievement of considera-

ble sophistication in their use. But the success of these
books depends more upon the habitual attitudes of a good
writer at the peak of his powers than upon the deliberate
organization of a private world-view: the constitution of a
Yoknapatawpha. Faulkner's Sanctuary (1931) expands land-
as-chronicle to contrast the slow actions of men rooted in
the land with the frantic haste of its despoilers. Eliot's
Waste Land motif is for Faulkner the index to a history of
wasteful action; and the horror of Temple Drake's rape with
a corncob functions symbolically as well, indicating by its
perversion of Nature her deprivation of naturalness. In
Light in August (1932), the contrast between the Lena Grove
and Joe Christmas parts of the book is achieved similarly:
Lena's movement is slow, heedless of mile-space or clock-
time; hence, artistic, even as the wagon which picks her up
is "like something moving forever and without progress
across an urn."12 Christmas, violent of movement, has
the "living earth against him" (367). While Christmas's rush
along "the street which was to run for fifteen years" (210)
ends in tragedy, Lena's symbolic attunement to the motion
of the planets--her "providential caution of the old earth of
and with and by which she lives" (23)--gradually pulls Hightower out of his world of shadows and twilight. Restraint
of the blood is a "crucifixion" (347), like the burden of
blackness of skin: the two are one, and both are eased
when Christmas is castrated. But Hightower is rewarded
for accepting Lena's pull to action by the vision of the continuity of history which Nature, through the August light of
the title, grants him (441-444, 466-467). From this masterful control Faulkner passed to Pylon (1935), which much like
To a God Unknown is a novel of excesses, using bleak city-
scape and swamp to make its point about sexuality.

     But Faulkner returns to greatness when he returns to
his County: Absalom, Absalom! (1936) identifies land and
the past in the mind of the anguished Quentin, and the book
is dominated by a figure, Sutpen, who attempts to shape the
land to his own purposes instead of accepting the land's con-
tours. But the land "tires" of Sutpen and then "destroys"
him, 13 his "innocence" the price paid for his determination
to carve an empire out of land which belonged to "anybody
and everybody" (221). Sutpens' raw sexual vigor stands in
stark relief against Rosa Coldfield's "female old flesh long
embattled in virginity" (7-8), but it is failure to respect sex
that partly accounts for his downfall, and themes of "blood"
that afflict his dynastic pretensions. At this point in Faulkner's career, the use of Nature-imagery to complement

characterization is fully-developed and authoritative.

At the same time, two little masterpieces indicate
Steinbeck's mature command of the same materials. Of
Mice and Men (1937) describes George and Lennie as sons
of Nature seeking freedom in Nature; the work's dramatic
interest thus stems from a logical desire for self-fulfill-
ment, though Lennie's wish for a cave "off in the hills" is
an ominous suggestion. Characters are united by a common dream whose actualization depends upon ownership of
land; ironically, their disappointment is accomplished through
affectionate "natural" slayings--first of a puppy, then of Curley's wife. Prefigured by a heron's killing of a snake, the
death of Lennie comes after he is tormented by the vision of
a giant rabbit, and the "fat of the land" credo is recited (a
consistent source of irony in Steinbeck). [14] Drama in Nature
also informs The Red Pony (1937), where Jody's initiation is
assisted by the pony named after the mountains of dreaming,
and whose death is a rough introduction to Nature's ways:
the savage fight for survival and freedom epitomized by the
buzzard Jody pathetically fights. Gitano's sense of the past
turns Jody from casual animal-killing to the foster-father-
hood of a new colt, delivered with the help of the "half
horse" Billy Buck (182). In the fourth section, the lessons
of Nature are applied to the situation of Grandfather, whose
painful awareness that "westering" is over and the "race of
giants" gone leads to a central statement of the American
condition and its inherent disappointments, using the land on
a continental scale (193-196, 198-200).

Similarly, Faulkner's The Unvanquished (1938) has its
correlative in geography: a model of the region, a child's
plaything. [15] The book tells of Bayard's rise to maturity,
foreshadowed by a gallop over a hill which leaves him "sus-
pended ... in a dimension without time in it"--the barrier
between childhood and manhood (75-76). As in The Red Pony,
American history is encapsuled in Bayard's life: the old
Sartoris code of right use of land plus revenge is purged of
violence by the War and other events, and becomes a new
Sartoris code largely concerned with Nature-values. And in
The Wild Palms (1939), the sound of the palms heralds the
discovery that grief is better than nothing; lacking a Mississippi setting, the title story relies upon animal imagery to
reach a point of insuring futurity through reconciliation with
land-values. "The Old Man" is a fantastic telescoping of
Genesis; its convict's entire lifetime is an experience
measured by the River and given value through it.

Textural similarities to The Wild Palms abound in
that true apotheosis of Grandfather's group-man, The Grapes
of Wrath (1939). A masterful balancing of forces, the novel
is paced with running descriptions of events befalling its
characters in terms of parallels in Nature. Observed
changes in a dried-up landscape welcome Tom Joad home,
and the stubborn turtle becomes his bestiary. The merging
of Nature-religion and group-man social activism, long important in Steinbeck's thinking, occurs when Jim Casy is
clearly described as a turtle-man. 16 Casy's Emersonian-
ism (32-33) includes a suspension of moral judgments (a
Nature-lesson which Steinbeck imposes on men as well, at
some cost in logic and credibility). The rape of the land is
opposed by the love of men for one another; therefore, "Manself" begins a westward trek (204-207). Casy's self-sacri-
fice as Christ of Nature results in Tom's separation from
his past in a ritual "coal-black cave of vines," from which
he emerges with the Christian promise to return in the spirit of the people (527, 551-553, 570-572). Rewriting the
Bible's flood, like Faulkner, Steinbeck has Rose of Sharon's
dead child sent afloat as a kind of Moses, with the mother
herself auguring future strength in her famous final gesture
of foster-motherhood (601-603, 609, 618-619). But even the
achievement of a masterpiece could not confirm Steinbeck's
happy arrangement of materials, as The Moon Is Down
(1942) demonstrates simply by changing to a foreign setting.

Actually, neither man performed well when he didn't
know the territory. Faulkner came home for The Hamlet
(1940), beginning a Snopes trilogy at every stage related to
Nature. Flem Snopes is characterized by a desire to own
things of Nature out of a lust after respectability, and in
the process employs a wild-horse swindle, land deals, and
the like, leaving a trail of "anger" in the earth. 17 The
impotent Flem's wasted field is his wife, Eula Varner,
whose initial description marks the apogee of Faulkner's
interest in sex: "... her entire appearance suggested some
symbology out of the old Dionysic times--honey in sunlight
and bursting grapes, the writhen bleening of the crushed
fecundated vine beneath the hard rapacious trampling goat-
hoof"[95].

Ike Snopes's idyll with the cow, described as a union
with cosmic history (186-189), prefigures Flem's eventual defeat at the hands of the Nature-related Eula and her daughter.
The negation of love--Lump Snopes profiting from Ike's
physical love for the cow, the impotent Flem marrying

(and thus desecrating) Eula--creates a cancer upon the earth
that three novels are required to remove.

Corresponding to The Hamlet in its use of idylls in a
world of animal bliss, and in its use of rampant sexuality,
respectively, are Cannery Row (1945) and The Wayward Bus
(1947). Indebted to the tide-pool research that gave Steinbeck his new invocation ("Our Father who art in nature ... ")
(363-364), Cannery Row presents casual death in Nature, the
sea's suggestion of death, a Doc "half Christ and half satyr"
(369-371): in short, a constant recrossing of the presumed
barriers between the human and animal worlds, somewhat
damaged by a mixing of levels of seriousness. An idyll like
the Carmel River frog-hunt becomes aria to the novel's re-
citative. The figure of Doc, isolated by his special understanding, is a counterpart to Faulkner's Gavin Stevens. The
Wayward Bus shows Steinbeck losing control over his set of
"meanings," and beginning to insert them as philosophical
decorations rather than as integral parts of his narrative.
Weighed down by a confused fabliau-as-exemplum presenta-
tion, this story of the bus of fools strains to present Juan
Chicoy as savior in Nature's religion: what remains of divine love after Christianity's decline. Here the California
landscape and its hints of sexuality give Steinbeck, like
Faulkner, a last nostalgic fling at allegorical sex. At the
end of his major period of work, Steinbeck is beginning to
yield up authority over his Nature-devices. The Pearl (1947)
is a happy exception. More clearly allegorical, it presents
fewer problems. The scorpion epitomizes a natural evil no
worse than the hunting that consumes fishes and mice. But
when Kino says that the pearl "has become my soul" (513),
he creates a false ideal that isolates him even from his
family. Steinbeck neatly presents the pearl in its dual aspects of precious natural growth and "gray and ulcerous"
malignancy (527). Nature appears here as music, as in Cup
of Gold.

I will not dwell on the later works of these men at
length. Decline is evident in both as each man grew mis-
trustful of fiction's ability to speak out unamplified. The
new public Faulkner's Intruder in the Dust (1947), exchanges
metaphor for direct rhetoric, juxtaposing the contemporary
South with the drama of character; so too, in a more for-
mally significant way, does Requiem for a Nun (1951), where
the real interest is in the dramatic conflict of region (the
interchapters) and character (the play proper). Digging in
the earth is important in Intruder, this time a positive act

helping save the land-related Lucas Beauchamp (whereas digging after "treasure" is an image of corruption in The Hamlet); in The Mansion (1959), Flem is violently purged from
the earth by a kinsman who is then welcomed back into the
bosom of Nature--literally.   But the late appearance of
Christ-myth in Requiem (late, that is, compared to Steinbeck)
foreshadows fuller development in A Fable (1954), where
Faulkner posits a future when there may be an "entire earth
one unbroken machined de-mountained dis-rivered expanse of
concrete paving protuberanceless by tree or bush or
house...."[16] Thus Faulkner is forced by the actuality of
historical development to adjust the land-covenant to a concept of continuity with Nature, in which good men are seen
as remaining faithful to the contract even when Nature's
presence is unseen.   To the end, moreover, Faulkner uses
Nature-images to signify moral worth.   The evil are characterized by imagery of insect, rodent, mud, metal; Popeye
is remembered in Requiem as "hybrid," "spider," "worm."[19]
Snopeses are "rats," "termites," "tigers," "snakes," "wild-
cats," or "wolves" in The Town.[20] Faulkner, then, consistently uses Nature to center his works, in which everything is finally about placing oneself for or against the eternal, immutable Law embodied in Nature.

       Steinbeck's Burning Bright (1950) is, like Requiem for
a Nun, a play in which form and language are in thrall to
conception and philosophy.   Here "blood" involves the trans-
ference of art from generation to generation.   Joe Saul's
suspicion that "a farmer or a sailor, or a lineless, faceless
Everyone" might share his trapeze artist's worries about
siring a son to carry on (his ancestors were "natural spirits"
living in "trees and streams," "in the wind and in the black
storms") makes him retreat like a "mole" into a "secret
cave."[21] Mordeen's pregnancy puts her in a class with
Faulkner's Lena, as her year rolls "over and over as the
earth rolls" while her baby grows within her (86-90).   Pre-
dicted shifts to farm and ocean settings, however, do not
quite support the message of planned promiscuity in parent-
hood. East of Eden (1952), like A Fable, deals with the
problem of maintaining human integrity in an age which has
tossed away old values; the cave in Nature has become a
willow tree.   Overblown and yet compelling in its very sweep
(again like A Fable), East of Eden ends with Lee exhorting
Adam to bless Cal, remembering man's need to be "free"
and better than "the beasts."[22] The ritualistic "Timshel!"
closing confirms Steinbeck in a new role: rewriter of his
own rewritten Bible, To a God Unknown.

Sweet Thursday (1954) and The Short Reign of Pippin
IV (1957) are late outbursts of comic spirit that parallel that
of Faulkner in The Reivers, though both are lesser works.
In Sweet Thursday, which like The Reivers even ends with
the redemption of a prostitute, Steinbeck nearly parodies
his own use of Nature-motifs; in Pippin, the humor is directed outward, but with an easy use of the old imagery.
Because Sweet Thursday shows a straining after effect and
Pippin is necessarily dated, both works have suffered neglect, 23 though it might be noted that they evidence a care-
lessness about Nature-imagery that is almost saddening, con-
sidering how well the device had served Steinbeck in the
past.

The final works are both, to my thinking, immensely
successful in most respects, but particularly in their swan-
song virtuosity with Nature-imagery. The Reivers (1962) is
a striking, relaxed achievement in comedy, in which the
narrative takes the form of a journey across land and back:
a perilous cycle in which redemption is worked, initiation
accomplished, and epiphany (another birth, this time to a
prostitute) sighted. Virtue is a horse-race and the past is
where it belongs, right in the middle of Now. The still
point of the turning world in Faulkner's fiction is the point
at which a character is affixed to the earth; from that point,
lines of narrative stretch to infinity.

A masterful use of land-imagery and a final triumph,
The Winter of Our Discontent shifts the scene to New England, returning like America and Americans to first principles. With a Hawthornian sense of pastness in a season
of conventional religious significance, Eastertide, Ethan Allen Hawley struggles with personal corruption--the temptation of theft and the "predator" Margie Young-Hunt, "a hunt-
ress, Artemis for pants"24--assisted by the Eden Timshel
motif, here the good wife Mary and a daughter who is pos-
terity. In his "little cave" in the Hawley dock, Ethan obeys
the talisman's order to go on living "else another light
might go out" (308-311)--Steinbeck's final attainment of the
moral stance of The Wild Palms and a return to the Merlin-
magic of Cup of Gold. Winter, then, is a balanced use of
Nature-imagery, the achievement after which Steinbeck
searched long and found only on occasion, often falling into
excess, compromising forms, or losing the sense of Nature's
presence. Like Faulkner, he could not do without it.

III

Mutual commentary by Faulkner and Steinbeck is slight, as I began by saying. Asked in 1947 for his "five most important contemporaries," Faulkner named Steinbeck fifth, but added, "I had great hopes for him at one time. Now I don't know."[25] By 1955 he had discarded Steinbeck, telling a Japanese interviewer that "Steinbeck is just a reporter, a newspaperman, not really a writer."[26] Besides the moral judgment inherent in Faulkner's description (Steinbeck would have accepted the title), the comment is interesting for the fact that Faulkner had taken Steinbeck off his personal list of significant "failures," writers grappling with the tragic limitations of their craft. Furthermore, Faulkner deliberately denied the validity of the group-man concept in any form.[27]

Steinbeck, on the other hand, retained a consistent charity in public utterances, especially when, under fire for daring to receive the Nobel Prize, he followed a statement of doubt as to his pre-eminent worthiness by developing the entirety of his address out of the elements of Faulkner's: "Literature was not promulgated by a pale and emasculated critical priesthood singing their litanies in empty churches-- nor is it a game for the cloistered elect, the tin-horn mendicants of low-calorie despair."[28] Lacking Faulkner's eloquence, attempting none, Steinbeck nevertheless seems to be taking his image here from Light in August and Hightower's thoughts about Tennyson. And in paying tribute to his "great predecessor" for being aware "of human strength as well as of human weakness" (Speech, p. 8), Steinbeck reveals his own compelling humility.

What Steinbeck suffered from, separating his work in terms of quality from Faulkner's, was partly the inability to see the insufficiency of treating Nature's relationship with men merely through the repetition of certain devices, rather than by developing--as Faulkner did--a set of valid prior assumptions about man and the land which his fiction might then illustrate. I am not praising the dynamics of uncritical pigeonholing in stressing the difference between device and method, and in emphasizing the importance of that difference to these two men. Perhaps in holding so long to the value of nonteleological thinking, Steinbeck lost both the category and the imperative. Certainly, there is a strong possibility that Steinbeck's evident desire never to write the same book twice helped to separate his work from Faulkner's in quality, for Faulkner saw himself as trying repeatedly to get one book written successfully. Steinbeck's achievements are, in the light of these possibilities, the more surprising.

Notes

1. This chapter represents an expansion of my article "From Oxford to Salinas: Comparing Faulkner and Steinbeck," Steinbeck Quarterly, Vol. II, No. 3 (Fall 1969), by means of materials from my unpublished doctoral dissertation "Land-Nostalgia in the Novels of Faulkner, Cather, and Steinbeck" (New York University, 1967). A portion of this chapter was read at the Steinbeck Conference in Corvallis, Oregon, April 17-18, 1970, as "Faulkner Land and Steinbeck Country."

2. Compare Jim Casy's "There ain't no sin and there ain't no virtue. There's just stuff people do" to the implications of Winter's final scene.

3. That they disappeared even from memory is suggested by his comments on prejudice in Travels with Charley, and the evolving use of Oriental wisdom for East of Eden shown in Journal of a Novel.

4. Collected by Carvel Collins as William Faulkner: Early Prose and Poetry (Boston, 1962), pp. 86-89. Page numbers for this and other primary sources will be parenthetically inserted in the text, subsequent to the first reference.

5. New York, 1953; pp. 17-18. I have used the most reliable current edition of Steinbeck's novels; in many cases only the Bantam paperback is in print.

6. Carvel Collins, ed. (New York, 1968), pp. 76-85.

7. New York, 1926; p. 151.

8. New York, 1927; p. 11.

9. New York, 1960; pp. 1-3.

10. As I Lay Dying (New York, 1964), p. 139.

11. The Sound and the Fury (New York, 1929, 1946), pp.
    217, 298.

12. New York, 1932; pp. 4-5.

13. New York, 1936; p. 12.

14. In The Short Novels of John Steinbeck (New York,
    1953), pp. 268-272; this volume also contains Tor-
    tilla Flat, The Red Pony, The Moon Is Down, Can-
    nery Row, and The Pearl.

15. New York, 1938; pp. 3-5.

16. New York, 1939; pp. 25-26.

17. New York, 1940; p. 350.

18. New York, 1959; pp. 352-354.

19. New York, 1951; pp. 145-146.

20. New York, 1957; pp. 40, 102, 106-107.

21. New York, 1962; pp. 14, 18, 21.

22. New York, 1952; pp. 599-602.

23. Just as A Fable translates the rhetoric of the Nobel
    Prize Address into fiction--a process of only partial
    assimilation of one form into another--Sweet Thurs-
    day repeats the philosophical stance of The Log from
    the Sea of Cortez, and the later portrait "About Ed
    Ricketts" clearly identifies the source of the charac-
    ter of Doc. However, Faulkner's works are merely
    the philosophical culmination of a career, while
    those of Steinbeck's are a stage in a continuing
    development, and may be related directly to the
    other works of his canon only at a certain critical
    peril.

24. New York, 1961; p. 20.

25. In "Classroom Statements at the University of Mississ-
    ippi, " Lion in the Garden: Interviews with William
    Faulkner, 1926-1962, ed. James B. Meriwether and
    Michael Millgate (New York, 1968), p. 58.

26. From <u>Faulkner at Nagano</u> (Tokyo, 1956), but reprinted
     in <u>Lion</u>, p. 91.

27. In <u>Faulkner in the University</u>, ed. Frederick L. Gwynn
     and Joseph L. Blotner (Charlottesville, Va., 1959),
     pp. 5, 242, 269.

28. <u>Speech Accepting the Nobel Prize for Literature</u> (New
     York, 1962), p. 7. Steinbeck's peculiar phrasing
     here (<u>mendicant</u> for <u>vendor</u>) seems to have sprung
     out of a desire to be consistent with Faulkner's
     metaphor.

3. STEINBECK AND ERNEST HEMINGWAY

Steinbeck and Hemingway: Suggestions for a Comparative Study
by Peter Lisca

From many points of view it seems inevitable that John Steinbeck and Ernest Hemingway should be closely associated in any critical survey of American fiction from the late twenties to the present, especially as these two figures are the foremost heirs of our naturalistic literary tradition. Thus they share attention in certain specialized as well as general studies of American literature. They are even sometimes examined in the same chapters of such books. But curiously they have very seldom been studied closely together for the purpose of yielding reciprocal illumination. The present essay assumes simply that such an interlocking examination of two writers with so broad a common base might lead to a sharper perception of each one's particular accomplishment, and proposes to suggest certain possible fruitful areas of inquiry.

To begin with the most obvious and least important, it is strange that two such thoroughly professional writers so much in the public eye should have left so little notice of each other. The first mention of Steinbeck recorded in the Baker biography is that in 1942 Hemingway "said emphatically that he would rather cut three fingers off his throwing hand than write such a book" as Bombs Away, Steinbeck's frank and successful propaganda effort for the U.S. Air Force. Two years later, dining out with Steinbeck in New York and meeting by accident with John O'Hara, Hemingway may have been expressing something when he disdainfully broke over his own head O'Hara's antique blackhorn walking stick, which had been a gift from Steinbeck, who was simply disgusted at the incident. Of course all the facts are not known yet in either case; but if Hemingway, who felt compelled to publicly attack the abilities and personalities of so many of his contemporaries, has left any further judgment of Steinbeck, it has not yet been generally noticed.

46

Although, on the other hand, Steinbeck did not much care to
enter into criticism of his fellow writers, some remarks
about Hemingway have come to light. The gist of all of
them is a sincere admiration.

To Covici of the Viking Press he wrote (c. February, 1939), "I'm convinced that in many ways he is the
finest writer of our time"; and later, to his friend Ed Shee-
han he confided, "I was afraid to read Hemingway until I
was well along. . . . I knew he would influence me. " He
thought so much of "The Butterfly and the Tank, " one of
Hemingway's Spanish Civil War stories, that he wrote to
the author, saying that it was "one of a very few finest
stories in all time. " Responding to my own suggestion
(1956) that certain passages of To a God Unknown (1933)
had been strongly influenced by the Hemingway style, Steinbeck replied that he "didn't read him until about 1940. "
This awareness of Hemingway as a fellow writer was ac-
companied by an interest in the personality. To Ed Shee-
han, he wrote that when Hemingway was reported dead in
Africa (1935), "I was stunned--held a sort of personal wake--
Hemingway was terribly worried about immortality. It was
a gnawing thing with him. " And to the same correspondent
he wrote that when Hemingway received the Nobel Prize in
1954 he, Steinbeck, was as pleased as if he had gotten it
himself.

The literary careers of Steinbeck and Hemingway hold
some basic differences, but also some interesting and perhaps more significant similarities. Hemingway started in
journalism with the Kansas City Star and the Toronto Star
and began writing seriously in Europe under the tutelage and
practical encouragement of such figures as Anderson, Pound,
Joyce, Stein, Fitzgerald, and others. But Steinbeck in California had no such help from the déjà arrivés. Thus Hemingway was better known in critical circles with the appearance of his first little book, Three Stories and Ten Poems
(Paris, 1923), than Steinbeck was in 1936 after the publication of four novels and several excellent short stories, including two parts of The Red Pony. Ironically, Hemingway,
who started his career in the capitals of Europe, lived most
of his life in such places as Key West, a finca in Cuba, and
a ranch in Idaho. He professed to detest New York and
never stayed there except for brief visits. Steinbeck, on
the other hand, moved from rural and small town California
to New York, where he lived the last twenty-four years of
his life. Yet Steinbeck the New Yorker never stimulated

the degree of public recognition as a personality of our time
that Hemingway, the geographic recluse, did. Whereas in his
early career Steinbeck did very little journalistic work, this
was a form of writing on which he leaned heavily from
World War II until the end of his life. And, except for a
few pieces in the 1930's (an article in Nation, a series of
seven reports for the San Francisco News) and some of his
war dispatches, that journalism is of a very low caliber.
But Hemingway did some distinguished work in this field
throughout his career, from his dispatches on the League of
Nations to his reports on bullfighting in 1960 and the post-
humous A Moveable Feast. Both writers won a Pulitzer
prize, Steinbeck for The Grapes of Wrath and Hemingway
for The Old Man and the Sea. Both also received the Nobel
Prize for literature, Hemingway in 1954, and Steinbeck in
1962.

     When we turn from this angle on the two writers' per-
sonal careers to the progression of their work, certain important similarities appear. Both writers have published
nonfiction books which are philosophically central to their
major work: Hemingway, Death in the Afternoon (1932) and
Green Hills of Africa (1935); Steinbeck, Sea of Cortez (1941).
What bullfighting and big game hunting are to one writer,
marine biology is to the other. Hemingway's love of Spain
led him to propaganda and documentary work in The Spanish
Earth (1937), and his personal efforts on behalf of the Loyalists. In The Forgotten Village (1941), Steinbeck turns to
propaganda and documentary to help the Mexican villages
come into the twentieth century. Within one year of each
other were published The Grapes of Wrath (1939) and For
Whom the Bell Tolls (1940), both again devoted to social
causes, both large novels, in some important senses epics,
and both perhaps their respective authors' peak artistic
achievements. In The Pearl (1947), Steinbeck reached the
end of a long line of development started with To a God Unknown (1933). In Kino's throwing the pearl back into the sea
Steinbeck returns man completely to the bosom of Nature,
very much as Santiago returns in The Old Man and the Sea
(1952), blessing birds, marlins, and even some sharks.
Both are short, poetic, highly symbolic works. Finally,
in Colonel Cantwell of Across the River and into the Trees
(1950) Hemingway returns to his earlier, younger embodi-
ments as Nick Adams and Frederick Henry in order to destroy them--symbolically, with that gesture on the bank of
the Basso Piave; and realistically in the death of Colonel
Cantwell. With essentially the same purpose, Steinbeck in

Sweet Thursday (1954) returns to Doc of Cannery Row and, symbolically at least, kills him off by cheapening his charac- ter and marrying him to the prostitute, Suzy. Neither writ- er returned again to those areas of their material.

Although thus unexpectedly similar in some of their materials, Steinbeck and Hemingway contrast strongly in others. Most obvious is the degree to which the two writers are autobiographically present in their work. Hemingway's presence, from the early stories to Across the River and into the Trees, has been so pronounced as to seriously ham- per an objective criticism and understanding of his work. Steinbeck, on the other hand, except for appearing quite di- rectly in East of Eden, has very little autobiographical pres- ence in his fiction--nothing approaching Nick Adams, Fred- erick Henry, Robert Jordan, and Colonel Cantwell.

If the period of their writing is divided into the nine- teen-twenties, the thirties, the forties, and the fifties, fur- ther interesting comparisons emerge. For example, Heming- way, while only three years older than Steinbeck (and gradu- ating from high school only two years earlier) seems a whole generation older by virtue of his participation in World War I and his involvement in the expatriate movement and the "lost generation." Although 1929 saw the appearance of Steinbeck's first novel (Cup of Gold) and only the second nov- el of Hemingway (A Farewell to Arms), the latter novel com- pleted an already solid fictional world about World War I and its aftermath created by the two editions of In Our Time (1924, 1925), and The Sun Also Rises (1926). This is an important part of our literary and cultural heritage, a world to which Steinbeck, except in passing (East of Eden), has no reference.

It is also interesting to observe, and surprising in view of the strong tendency to identify Steinbeck's work with the proletarian movement of the thirties, that in fact not un- til 1936, with In Dubious Battle, a great strike novel, did he publish any proletarian fiction. Cup of Gold, The Pas- tures of Heaven, To a God Unknown, The Red Pony, and Tortilla Flat (all published during the Great Depression) had no reference to the current social scene. It was partly this lack of reference which made the latter novel so difficult to publish in 1935. While not as obviously proletarian as Stein- beck's strike novel, Hemingway's To Have and Have Not was published in book form only a year after the strike novel; and it was he, not Steinbeck, who in that year addressed

the Second American Writers' Congress. Of the seven books
of fiction Steinbeck published in the 1930's, only two, perhaps three, are concerned with the depression, and perhaps
one of the stories in The Long Valley. If, in a strictly
limited sense, Hemingway's personal interest in the Spanish
Loyalist cause can be called a proletarian one, then with his
film documentary, his reporting, his play The Fifth Column,
several short stories and For Whom the Bell Tolls, his involvement in the political-social realities of the 1930's can
be seen as comparable to Steinbeck's, although the latter's
involvement was entirely American.

        Although both writers served as journalists in World
War II (Hemingway, of course, in a more flamboyant manner), neither produced a novel using the war as major material. Steinbeck's The Moon Is Down (1942) can be identified with that war only by inference, purposefully so; Hemingway deals with that war but briefly through the reveries
of Colonel Cantwell in Across the River and Into the Trees
(1950) and the Caribbean manhunt of Hudson in Islands in the
Stream. Of the two writers only Steinbeck, in The Winter
of Our Discontent (1961), has produced a work of fiction dealing
directly with post-World War II society, particularly in
America.

        But then another contrast between the two writers is
that Hemingway has seldom written about America at all,
except in some early stories and To Have and Have Not. Although his major protagonists (except Santiago) are Americans,
they live, or at least act, in Europe. Steinbeck, on the
other hand, excluding his first novel--a historical romance--
has set none of his major fiction outside the United States,
unless one excepts The Pearl, certainly not Pippin IV. In
this connection it is pertinent to remark that of the two authors it is Steinbeck who in his fiction almost always gives
us the sense of physical communities; and they may be as
various as those in The Pastures of Heaven, Tortilla Flat,
The Grapes of Wrath, and The Winter of Our Discontent.
With few exceptions (in some early stories, To Have and
Have Not) Hemingway presents us with a community which is
not so much physical as it is spiritual--an "in" group, whether they be a lost generation, fellow army officers, aficiona-
dos, hunters, guerrillas, etc. This difference is vitally related to the phenomenon that one tends to recall Steinbeck's
fiction in terms of themes and Hemingway's in terms of
characters.

Thus proportionately much more of the criticism has
dealt with Hemingway's characters than with Steinbeck's.
Certain comparisons, however, can be made. Both writers
have been accused of creating animal-like characters on a
very low level of morality and ratiocination. There is not
adequate space to discuss these familiar arguments here; but
it should be pointed out, first, that both writers have created
characters of considerable moral and intellectual sophistica-
tion--Jake Barnes, Robert Jordan, Colonel Cantwell; and Dr.
Burton, Ethan Hawley, Doc, Samuel Hamilton, Lee. Second-
ly, those characters not of this intellectual caliber are employed very skillfully by both writers to reveal with great
force significant aspects of human life not so readily accessi-
ble in more sophisticated personalities. Another similarity
in their respective characters is the extent to which both
writers admire in them skillfullness and knowledge. In
Steinbeck, the whole gamut of his admiration appears in The
Wayward Bus, from auto mechanic to stripteaser. In Hemingway this is equally obvious in his good soldiers, fisher-
men, or even economics professors (To Have and Have Not).
Related to this admiration in both writers is the frequent
mentor-neophyte relationship between characters, as for example Santiago-the boy, Colonel Cantwell-Renata and Casy-
Tom, Billy Buck-Jody. In both novelists the mentor figure
sometimes appears alone or in but brief contact with the neo-
phyte, as in Hemingway's Count Greffi and Count Mippopo-
lous, Steinbeck's various hermits and "seers." The two
writers are also similar in some ways in their treatment of
women and the relationship between men and women. In
Hemingway, perhaps only Brett and Pilar achieve real independence, and they seem to do so at the price of their femi-
ninity. And although Hemingway writes much more than
Steinbeck about sexual love, it is the latter who most often
presents married women sympathetically. Both writers frequently present a close male companionship, such as that of
Jake and Bill or George and Lennie. Apropos of Lennie, it
is interesting that Steinbeck should, like Faulkner, so frequently use characters whom, as he describes Tularecito,
"God has not quite finished." There is hardly a novel that
does not contain a sub-normal character. Hemingway, on
the other hand, eschews this kind of character completely,
but does create and effectively use a variety of homosexual
characters with surprising frequency. There is perhaps one
homosexual in all of Steinbeck's work.

Related to this point is Steinbeck's long sustained interest in psychology, particularly the Jungian school, which

is most important in his work before 1950. Significantly,
his interest in Freudian psychology is associated with his
later, least successful novels including East of Eden, Sweet
Thursday, and The Winter of Our Discontent.

   Certainly a major difference between these two authors' works is that existing between their heroes. In Hemingway, even Robert Jordan, the most committed and engaged
of his heroes, is yet in an important sense an outsider, a
longer pursuing essentially personal goals. The distinguish-
ing mark of practically all Steinbeck heroes is their leadership and complete involvement in a communal action. There
is another important difference which is almost a similarity.
In Hemingway, the hero's action frequently demonstrates that
a man may be destroyed but not defeated; in Steinbeck, that
a man frequently survives, but does not succeed; dreams,
but does not accomplish.

   Style, of course, in all its aspects, is a major point
of comparison, although it is the most difficult to discuss
adequately here. Steinbeck uses a much greater variety of
prose styles than does Hemingway, who really has variations
on only one style. But in some short stories and such novels as In Dubious Battle, Of Mice and Men, and The Pearl
there is much ground for comparison. Steinbeck's prose is
hardly ever the iceberg seven-eights under the surface that
Hemingway describes as his own ideal. Hemingway does
make much more use of implication, the spaces made meaningful by the author's firm knowledge of what is left out. But
both writers have reached a large popular audience in part because of a deceptively simple surface and their ability to
write in terms of sensations, although here it is Steinbeck
who is more often abstract. It is no accident that both men
have expressed a preference for the music of Bach, and in
those works which are most successful the dimensionality is
an effect of clean counterpoint and not of massed chords.

   Symbolism is very important in both writers, also,
and the differences in its nature and purpose revealing.
Both make extensive use of natural objects as symbols, and
of animals, such as mice, turtles, bulls, fish, ducks; also,
both use landscape for this purpose, and climate--mountains,
gulfstream, swamp, rain, snow, drought, valleys, tidepools,
caves. An important difference, however, is that Steinbeck,
in addition, moves much more frequently for his symbols
into the worlds of literature, legend, and myth, some novels taking their basic structure therefrom--Tortilla Flat

(Mort d'Arthur), In Dubious Battle (Paradise Lost), The Grapes of Wrath, East of Eden (the Bible), and others. He thus creates a "fourth dimension" of external reference different from that of Hemingway, whose own is achieved by what Malcom Cowley calls "rituals or strategies," "rites and ceremonies," and remains within the work itself.

Another point of contrast in style between the two writers is their use of narrative point of view. This is closely related to differences in the nature and role of their hero figures, as discussed above. With the exception of his last novel, Steinbeck employs only third person more or less objective point of view narration. Hemingway, however, uses varieties of first person narration extensively and also experiments with mixing or merging points of view. There is a philosophical as well as formal significance here.

Finally, we come to those comparisons perhaps most important, but difficult to disengage entirely from those matters of style and materials discussed above. And here we return to these two writers' common ground as heirs of literary naturalism. While Hemingway has never abandoned, but consistently modified, this inheritance, Steinbeck, although contributing much in his early work, has since The Wayward Bus moved steadily away from it toward a view and value system essentially suburban-Christian. Thus Hemingway in his last novel, The Old Man and the Sea, arrives at an almost mystic acceptance of man's consanguinity with all of Nature very similar to that out of which Steinbeck wrote, before 1947, such disparate works as The Grapes of Wrath and To a God Unknown. Santiago, in fact, is reminiscent of Joseph Wayne in the latter novel (1933). Until this change in Steinbeck, however--and some remnants of the earlier view persist, fossilized, in later works--this common inheritance of the two writers led to another important similarity--that between Hemingway's stoic acceptance of a deterministic, indifferent universe, and Steinbeck's non-teleological thinking, as it is defined in Sea of Cortez.

Other corollaries follow. Both writers often present man in situations of violence. But whereas the Hemingway hero frequently makes a career or avocation of such violence, whether hunting, bullfighting, boxing, running contraband, or soldiering, in Steinbeck's fiction (with the exception of the "Cain" figures in East of Eden, in whom it is seen as a curse) the characters engage in violence only for survival or for some communal goal, as an unavoidable contingency.

They are capable of great violence when necessary, but do
not seek it out as do Hemingway's characters sometimes,
as the author has stated about his own adventures, to avoid
doing violence to themselves. This contrast between the
two writers is pointed up hilariously in the account of a
hunt for big-horn sheep in Sea of Cortez.

But despite this difference about violence, both writers are notable for the depth of aesthetic feeling touched by
this Nature and their great ability to express it; and both
also present man as incomplete apart from intimate contact
with that world. Here Hemingway (except for Santiago)
stops, with Nature as sensation and physical discipline. But
Steinbeck goes on to a scientific engagement with Nature as
well, while at the same time speculating earnestly on pan-
theistic, quasi-religious relationships. This contrast is to
be expected in two authors of whom one (in Green Hills of
Africa) rejects the "small, dried" minds of the nineteenth
century American transcendentalists, and the other accepts
as one of the major sources of his thinking in his greatest
novel--The Grapes of Wrath.

The foregoing points of comparison between these two
writers might well be extended. But perhaps the exploratory
purpose of this essay has been achieved. Of necessity, some
of the points seem over-simplified; to develop adequately
even a few of the most important would require a book-
length study. The value of pursuing further some of the
comparisons, however, seems clear. For, as certain obvious differences between the two writers have tended to ob-
scure the much more important similarities, so have their
obvious similarities eclipsed some essential differences.

4. STEINBECK AND NIKOS KAZANTZAKIS

Steinbeck, Kazantzakis and Socialism*
by Andreas K. Poulakidas

Concentrating one's intellectual powers to evaluate
and analyze the creative process of a novelist, to compare
and contrast his works, his early and late inspiration, worthy
and honorable though it may be, has provincial and narrow
limitations which prevent the critic from looking at literature
as a whole; and one merely speaks about it in social and
moral terms: "popular and good, popular and bad, unpopular and good, unpopular and bad."[1] To define literature as
literature, as a cultural phenomenon, in its comparative,
natural, and universal perspective means to transcend the
egotistic logic of the new critics who anesthetize the work
itself and then start dissecting. The work is what the critic
who lives in a state of self-imposed grace means it to be,
and its creator, sinful from the start for his creative urge,
is found, euphemistically, outside of lasting grace, and,
metaphysically, outside of time and space. The critic exists
and not the author. What may spare us from such an escha-
tological day is, on a more sophisticated level, the comparative approach which prevents epistemologically the critic
from saying he is more knowledgeable than the author and
which bestows on the author a half-divine presence which
does not get in the way of the critic, and which cannot be
ignored. However, there is an omnipresence that the saint-
ly critic and the sinful author acknowledge, and this is culture: bigger than both, bolder than either, brighter than all.
"By an ideology," Kenneth Burke baroquely states,

> is meant the nodus of beliefs and judgments which
> the artist can exploit for his effects. It varies

*Based on a paper read at the 1969 MMLA Conference at
St. Louis in the comparative literature section.

from one person to another, and from one age to
another, but insofar as its general acceptance
and its stability are more stressed than its particular variations from person to person and from
age to age, an ideology is a 'culture.'[2]

The comparative approach becomes, I would say, the agnos-
tic approach to both creativity and criticism, because the
critic in the dark hopes to produce new and greater light by
rubbing two matched authors together. It is comparable in
Burkean terms to "a kind of aesthetic mysticism" which includes the following: "(1) the heart-conscious kind of listen-
ing, or vigilance, that precedes expression; (2) the expression in its unguarded simplicity; (3) modification of the expression, in the light of more complicated after-thoughts."[3]

        Thus, it profits not the agnostic critic to say that
The Grapes of Wrath is far superior to In Dubious Battle
and The Greek Passion far better than The Fratricides,
because he is not true to himself. He can only doubt what
something is, until he intuitively grasps its first causes.
And there is a plethora of lost critics who have been able
to judge Steinbeck's good deeds and his wicked works; Peter
Lisca in his article, "Steinbeck's Image of Man and His Decline as a Writer," makes no pretentions about Steinbeck's
work: "Steinbeck's decline as a writer of major or even
serious fiction is a phenomenon which has been asserted
often enough to need no emphasis here."[4]   Perhaps Kazantzakis will also have such critics as Lisca.   Kazantzakis'
Greek Passion and Fratricides, even a sophomoric comparatist
will tell one, have qualitative differences: one is better than
the other.   Fratricides lacks to a certain degree the artistic
polish, the transitional smoothness, the unity and direction,
the complexity of plot that Greek Passion has been blessed
with even though Fratricides, written in 1949, a year after
Greek Passion, would be expected from an evolutionist's
point of view to be a better novel.   Maybe this is why Fratricides was not published until after Kazantzakis' death.
And even an amateur would inform one that these two novels
of Kazantzakis are far better than these two of Steinbeck's
on the mere phenomenon of his present popularity; and no
Nobel Prize was given to Kazantzakis. Logically, the comparative method does not do much on this level. It may
point out certain features of the work itself, but it fails to
see the works as a whole and to relate them to a greater
whole, as products of a cultural phenomenon which treats
literature as literature.

One plays the numbers game when one speculates whether Kazantzakis had read Steinbeck's novels written in the late thirties. If this be true, one can merely add a footnote to the critic's observation of the surprisingly great cerebral identity of these two novelists. Steinbeck and Kazantzakis were once both journalists, and the touch of reporting the news, presenting the bare facts with some literary dexterity, can be clearly noticed in Kazantzakis' Toda Raba and sporadically in The Fratricides; it is most obvious in Steinbeck's In Dubious Battle. Both apparently were motivated by their times to write what they saw, Steinbeck by the economic depression of the thirties in America, and Kazantzakis by the civil war and political chaos in Greece at the end of World War II. Again, both were wooed by a similar political ideology (which throughout their lifetime they did not totally and exclusively embrace) and in whose spokesman, Lenin, they acknowledged a new Savior of the masses. Kazantzakis in his autobiography reveals this:

> Yes, Lenin was another new savior, I reflected, another new savior created by the enslaved, hungry, and oppressed to enable them to bear slavery, hunger, and oppression--another new mask for mankind's despair and hope. [5]

Thus one cannot comprehend these writers merely on their works themselves, nor on the basis of their oscillating political convictions, but on something greater than themselves or their works which makes these novelists such twins, such comrades in culture. Kenneth Burke puts it as follows: "men build their cultures by huddling together, nervously loquacious, at the edge of an abyss. "[6] And this abyss for both is their interest in socialism. Culture is that heritage of man that makes him, his works, and his fellowman what they are. In studying them and the causes which triggered their works, we are not singularly defining them, nor their works per se, but culture as a whole, i. e. , the cause, the agent, and the effect, their acts; and this in its entirety is what culture is: a phenomenon that can be better approached through the comparative method, which takes into consideration more causes and more effects. To look only at the work itself, one has criticism; to examine only the author himself, one has biography; to compare literatures, one has a greater reality: culture.

Usually a necessary component of the novel is its

dramatic tension or conflict, and the form of the above four
novels being considered here is based on the established historical observation of class struggle. This is not so much
a conflict between good and bad (although the author's ideological propensity or his lack of propensity may signify
where his sympathies lie), between self and society, between
male and female, but for these novels it is a clear dichotomy
and antagonism between two classes of society: the right
and the left, the haves and the have-nots, the established
and the non-established; or in more concrete terms, between
the communists and the capitalists, the socialists and the
loyalists. These novels seem to substantiate Burke's observation that a given ideology can only have a given form,
and it is this form, undeniably determined by time as it was,
that has pre-established itself on these novels--a fact that
the authors, original or dependent, had little control over,
just as romance often takes place because there is a full
moon.

> And similarly, throughout the permutations of his-
> tory, art has always appealed, by the changing in-
> dividuations of changing subject-matter, to certain
> potentialities of appreciation which would seem to
> be inherent in the very germ-plasm of man, and
> which, since they are constant, we might call in-
> nate forms of the mind. [7]

In In Dubious Battle, the strikers, organized by the "reds,"
by Mac and Jim, are seeking their rights for more humane
wages from the Fruit Growers' Association of California
that expects the migrants to work for nothing and that shows
no compassion for human misery and pain. In The Grapes
of Wrath, the polarization is clear, and it is the story of a
family that is deprived of their land in Oklahoma by an impersonal and greedy "monster" and that heads to California,
the promised land, only to find there more exploitation and
degradation. They are at the mercy of rich landlords who,
through their instruments of law and order, are able to sup-
press them and thousands of other migrants.

Kazantzakis, in his Greek Passion, has two distinct
communities opposing each other, one comprised of Greeks
driven away from their homes in the Bosporus by the Turks,
and the other of well-to-do Greeks of Lycovrissi who drive
away their suffering brethren into the caves of Sarakina, in
order to protect their own material interests threatened by
their hungry and landless compatriots. The idea of two en-

campments is also found in Kazantzakis' Fratricides in which
the two warring factions are the reds and the blacks, the
communists and nationalists, a force of guerrillas hiding in
the mountains and a force of government troops trying to
protect a God-forsaken hamlet. The authors visualize society and man as divided and classified according to his political ideology, which has been cultivated by his human condition: hunger or satiety.

This observation leads these novelists, then, to consider how Christianity responds to this human condition, and
Christianity cannot be ignored by them since the human condition in the Western world has also been nurtured by Christ.
Kazantzakis realizes this even more, because he is aware
of the homogeneous religious faith of his countrymen. Christ
is conceived by both writers to be on the side of the suffering masses, and is counted among those who witness the injustice and inhumanity around them. Consequently, Christ
is usually identified and associated with those rebels who
seek a better world with more justice, equality, and freedom. Doc, Joy, and Jim in In Dubious Battle, along with
Casy, the preacher, in The Grapes of Wrath, are comparable to Kazantzakis' Manolios, priest Fotis, and Father Yanaros who side with the oppressed and who have a Christ-like
image. At the time of Casy's murder, Steinbeck has him
displaying forbearance, like Christ, to his enemies by saying: "You fellas don't know what you're doin'. "[8] And Manolios' voluntary sacrifice, symbolically in the Church and on
Christmas day, is anticipated only moments before by his
confession: "If bolshevik means what I have in my spirit,
yes, I am a bolshevik ...; Christ and I are bolsheviks. "[9]

Kazantzakis uses his characters as vehicles in presenting the Marxist point of view. His clergymen are socialists in disguise who interpret Christ and Christianity in socialistic terms as Father Yanaros does in The Fratricides
when he says: "I say it and I repeat: the real Christ
walks with the people, struggles with them, is crucified
with them, is resurrected with them"; and later when he
goes on to say: "He is here on earth, fighting, He, too,
feels pain. He, too, faces injustice; He starves and is
crucified along with us. "[10] Father Yanaros is by no means
a conventional priest who speaks in generalities and is content in chanting and swinging the thurible, in believing that
religion and tradition are safeguarded by the old order.
Christ, for him, as a living and vibrant spiritual force of
his time, is associated with the spirit of the young monk

60

who has joined the communists in their efforts to eliminate
injustice, and this emaciated monk comes as a contrast to
the obese monk, who exploits the religious sentiments of the
villagers by asking them to pray before the alleged Holy
Sash of the Virgin Mother.   Father Yanaros' indignation toward this depraved monk is balanced out by his calm and
brotherly dialogue with the red-inclined, educated, and de-
posed monk, Brother Nicodemus, who has realized that Lenin
is "The Great Comforter," the Paraclete, "sent unto you
from the Father, even the Spirit of truth."[11] Yet, when he
goes to explain his faith to the communist guerrillas, they
laugh and taunt him, abuse and ostracize him, and he finds
himself alone and wounded.   The faith and mission of this
monk are gradually espoused by Father Yanaros who is also
deceived by the communists and in the end killed.

Such a contrast is also found in The Greek Passion
between Priest Fotis and Priest Grigoris.   In writing his
dissertation, "Christ, Freedom and Kazantzakis," Michael
A. Anthonakes observed the kinship of thought of these two
novelists, when, regarding The Grapes of Wrath and The
Greek Passion, he wrote:

> Both novels have a Christ figure, a heroic priest-
> minister, a Magdalene earth mother--all of whom
> are involved in an attempt to help a displaced
> group move peacefully into an established culture.
> The reaction to Steinbeck's work has also revealed
> that there are many forces in society that do not
> criticize a novel as an art form.   When an institu-
> tion feels that its position is threatened, it reacts.
> The Associated Farmers of Kern County, California
> called the book communist propaganda; the Holy
> Synod in Athens did the same for The Greek Pas-
> sion.   And Steinbeck, interestingly enough, who
> has not fared too well with critics in the United
> States, commands a great respect throughout
> Europe. [12]

Manolios in The Greek Passion assists Priest Fotis.   The
same relationship can be seen with Jim in In Dubious Battle
who serves as Mac's assistant and with Tom in The Grapes
of Wrath who acts as a disciple to preacher Casy; and yet,
Manolios is a fuller, more integrated character, a combina-
tion of all three of Steinbeck's characters, Doc, Joy, and
Jim, without, however, the aggressive instincts of Jim.
Tom, more differentiated than the other Steinbeck charac-

ters, still lacks the characterization that would enable him
to live as a memorable character. Also, Father Yanaros
and Priest Fotis are more solid characters than Casy, who
seems to be motivated by whims, by accidental occurrences,
rather than by his own volition and belief in a better world.
Thus, good and evil, in a political sense, are better defined
and more sharply contrasted by Kazantzakis, who depicts
those forces that oppose the refugees not as an impersonal
and abstract power structure that is only sensed through its
forces of law and order, but as the mean Priest Grigoris
and his church elders, who use strong language against the
refugees and their sympathizers:

> Bolsheviks! You receive orders from Moscow to
> overthrow religion, country, the family and proper-
> ty, the four great pillars of the world! Manolios,
> curse him, is your leader. And Priest Fotis has
> come from the other end of the world bringing, by
> way of a new Gospel, Moscow's orders![13]

The community of Sarakina finally has no other alternative
except to be militant and to seek through confrontation its
rights from the community and church at Lykovrissi. Steinbeck concludes his two novels in the same fashion. His
characters have no other choice except to rely on strife and
violence.

    In many respects, these novels are identical. Stein-
beck's response, however, to the communist movement in In
Dubious Battle is not very strong. From lack of conviction
or from fear or from lack of technical know-how, his reds
are little more successful than Conrad's Verloc and his gang
or Dostoyevsky's Verhovesky Jr. and his group of subver-
sives. He depicts them in an objective manner, and wants
to show how radical, irrational, and cruel they can be; and
yet, secretly and inwardly, he seems to revel in the communist ideology and mission. He is not as successful as Kazantzakis in criticizing the party machinery as an unredeemed
agency with the same human weaknesses and at the same
time in admiring the communist ideology as Kazantzakis was
able to do in The Fratricides. Steinbeck's failure in not
creating real characters may lie in the fact that he considers the political situation to be far more important than politically oriented characters. What he seems to be doing is
portraying the times, innumerable incidents of human cruelty
rather than the honest response of individuals to a given ideology. He does not seem to be concerned with the rebels who may

resemble Christ as much as he is with the many circumstances and incidents that can trigger confrontation and violence.
The murders of Joy, Doc, and Jim are exploited by Mac as
reasons for revolt rather than as reasons to show the tragedy
of several persons who have value as individuals and who
represent and live greater theological and metaphysical
truths.

Thus, almost half of The Grapes of Wrath is the
journey to the promised land, where, hour by hour and day
by day, there are happenings that develop Casy's and Tom's
realization that the present inhumane system can only be
overcome through subversion and violence.   Kazantzakis
quickly dispenses with the refugees' journey and brings them
to the place where great heroes emerge and carry the cross
of Lenin.   Their immediate opponents are not the civil au-
thorities, but the prospering community, real and tangible.
Their sympathizers are also very visible and develop out of
this confrontation.   Kazantzakis' characters are torn apart
many times by their own inner conflict, whereas Steinbeck's
fight only an external enemy and are obsessed with their
poverty and destitution, the "strictly biological image of
man. "[14]   Steinbeck's characters are always on the move;
and when they reach a certain point in the narrative, they
quietly disappear or quickly die, and this occurs to Doc,
Joy, and Dick in In Dubious Battle and to Connie, Al, Noah,
Tom, and Casy in The Grapes of Wrath.

Steinbeck sees the capitalistic system so well-en-
trenched and so all-powerful that all opposing trends and
subversions are simply dissolved, and nothing becomes of
them.   Steinbeck does not really believe that communism
will succeed in the United States, whereas Kazantzakis' novels bear the possibility and chance that this sytem may prevail in Greece as it did in other countries of Eastern Europe.
On the other hand, Steinbeck seems to be pointing out to the
capitalists what turns man into a communist, with the hope
that social evils will be corrected by those responsible in
the first place, for allowing them to exist.   He hopes the
establishment will hearken to his warning as the Kerner Commission and the Walker Report hope that society and government, local and national, will realize the causes of violence
and will remedy them.   Through his stark naturalism and
blunt photography of the American free enterprise system,
he hopes that the capitalist will modify his ways and inject
some idealism into his materialism and commercialism and
that the sociologists' warning may be heeded by America if she

is to survive. His would-be communists are not idealists,
but naturalists and pragmatists, who are concerned primarily
with practical things: repairing cars, finding food for the
family, keeping the camp clean, delivering babies, giving
enemas, caring for the aged, burying the dead, and doing
all those things that any good democratic institution "with
charity for all" would naturally do.

Contrarily, Kazantzakis' would-be communists are
idealists, reborn in Christ through Lenin and unanointed in
an age of technology, big government, taxation, and affluence,
which makes man's existence complex and terrifying, and social legislation a necessary evil. Kazantzakis' Christian socialists preach a better world which they visualize can come
about for all people whose only problem is not an evil nature, since they have been reborn in Christ, but hunger.
Spiritual birth is a necessary concomitant for any social
progress, and those communists who do not follow Christ's
spirit of love are not any different than the capitalists.
Steinbeck opposes the misery produced by man who takes
advantage of his fellow man; and Chapter Seven of The Grapes
of Wrath exposes adequately the American businessman's cru-
dity and bluntness, and in this instance, that of the used-car
dealer whose philosophy of life is to "sock it to 'em."[15]
Controls, programs, legislation, welfare, and concern, Steinbeck says, are needed. This is his warning to America.
Injustice, inhumanity, and hunger create and promote the
Marxist ideology:

> If you who own the things people must have could
> understand this, you might preserve yourself. If
> you could separate causes from results, if you
> could know that Paine, Marx, Jefferson, Lenin,
> were results, not causes, you might survive. But
> that you cannot know. For the quality of owning
> freezes you forever into 'I,' and cuts you off for-
> ever from the 'we.'[16]

Steinbeck's romanticism has barely a chance to come
to life, because his naturalistic settings and circumstances
overpower his characters; and romanticism implies a hope
in change, and is not concerned with warnings, preventive
action, shocking dramatization, all entitled corrective meas-
ures--the objective of the naturalist. Changes in the political and social structure, Steinbeck seems to say, are determined by biological necessity and not by ideological theories. Consequently, Steinbeck's view of socialism is lo-

calized, narrowed down to the needs of the suffering American, whereas Kazantzakis conceives socialism as a movement with a broader scope, a more universal setting. His
social realism is mythical and heroic, figuratively depicted
as "a strange new god," as "a flame" that is engulfing all
mankind whose former saviors, Christ, Mohammed, and
Buddha, are now wearing the mask of Lenin. Steinbeck has
Casy hearing

> 'a movin', an' a sneakin', an' a rustlin' an'--an'
> a res'lessness. They's stuff goin' on that the
> folks doin' it don't know nothin' about--yet. They's
> gonna come somepin' outa all these folks goin' wes'
> --outa all their farms lef' lonely. They's gonna
> come a thing that's gonna change the whole coun-
> try.'17

This movement for Steinbeck, if it implies a new social system or more socialistic legislation, is only a national phenomenon and affects only the deprived man in the United
States; and it is even implied that the unionization of the
American working man will solve his problems. However
much his characters suffer--and if this could be measured,
I would venture to guess that Steinbeck's characters are
made to suffer more than Kazantzakis'--Steinbeck's social
realism is a provincial one, a chauvinistic, non-idealistic
one. Many of his starving hordes of the thirties have probably become the bigoted, self-centered, self-contented, callous
upper and middle classes of the sixties, secure in unionism
and oblivious to human suffering and injustice, unless it is,
of course, found in their very backyard; most unfortunately,
they have become oblivious to their shoeless days and hungry
hours.

Michael Anthonakes disagrees with Markos Augeres
who feels that "the American novel has something in common with Kazantzakis"; and this is Kazantzakis' "primitive
exoticism," his "love of the hard, the primitive, the wild,
the instinctual" that has made Kazantzakis very popular in
America. Anthonakes rightly points out throughout his dissertation that Kazantzakis' Christ puts great demands on
man, creates tremendous psychic pressures and inner con-
flicts for his followers, whereas "the Western hero is totally devoid of inner spiritual torment." Furthermore, he adds:

> Nor can one easily see any similarity between
> Kazantzakis' primitive exoticism and the hardness

of American realists. When one thinks of Hemingway, Steinbeck and Dreiser, he finds that Kazantzakis has a rhetorical lushness and a highly-
wrought subjectivity that is foreign to the American
novel. If anything, to an American, Kazantzakis'
technique is rather romantic and old-fashioned, and
one has to turn to an early form of the American
novel for something similar. [18]

Both critics are right and wrong. Certainly, Kazantzakis'
style is not like that of the American realists nor like that
of Steinbeck's in particular; however, Kazantzakis' subject-
matter is very similar. It shows his concern for the suffering masses.

Regardless of the texture of their vision of social
realism or socialism, Steinbeck and Kazantzakis have, in
spite of their qualitative differences, other themes in these
works which can only further validate their cultural comrade-
ship. Both display a strong sense of sympathy and pity for
woman who seems to suffer more than man. Their works
bear innumerable anti-intellectual barbs, and the Oriental
point of view is also not absent. Both tend to agree that a
dynamic and vibrant Christianity is that which has aligned
itself with suffering mankind. Both experience the same social problems of their age; and their culture, different stylistically and ethnically though it may be, shares in the
same fermentation. Their literature cannot but be related
and very close in spirit--and one need not be necessarily
the legal parent of a certified and documented offspring.

Notes

1. Kenneth Burke, Counter-Statement (Chicago: University
   of Chicago Press, 1953), p. 91.

2. Ibid. , p. 161.

3. Ibid. , pp. 213-14.

4. Peter Lisca, Modern Fiction Studies, 11 (1965), 3.

5. Nikos Kazantzakis, Report to Greco, trans. P. A.
   Bien (New York: Simon and Schuster, 1965), p.
   369.

6. Burke, p. 215.

7. Ibid. , p. 46.

8. John Steinbeck, The Grapes of Wrath (New York:
    Modern Library, 1939), p. 527.

9. Nikos Kazantzakis, The Greek Passion, trans. Jona-
    than Griffin (New York: Simon and Schuster, 1965),
    p. 426.

10. Nikos Kazantzakis, The Fratricides, trans. Athena
    Gianakas Dallas (New York: Simon and Schuster,
    1964), pp. 22, 25.

11. Ibid. , p. 66.

12. Michael A. Anthonakes, "Christ, Freedom, and Kazant-
    zakis, " Ph. D. dissert. , New York University, 1965,
    p. 191.

13. Kazantzakis, The Greek Passion, p. 311.

14. Lisca, p. 7.

15. Steinbeck, The Grapes of Wrath, p. 83.

16. Ibid. , p. 206.

17. Ibid. , p. 237.

18. Anthonakes, pp. 149-50.

5. STEINBECK AND D. H. LAWRENCE

The God in the Darkness: A Study of John Steinbeck and
D. H. Lawrence
by Richard F. Peterson

When John Steinbeck expressed his admiration for
D. H. Lawrence, he was acknowledging a writer who had an
intense effect upon him for a brief period of time. [1] Lawrence's general influence on Steinbeck was not so pervasive
that Steinbeck's writing continually reflects Lawrencean
themes or that the careers of the two men coincide in terms
of the development of their fiction.   Instead, as Peter Lisca
points out, in To A God Unknown and in many of the stories
in The Long Valley, Steinbeck seems preoccupied with psychological interests that reflect a possible reading of D. H.
Lawrence. [2] It is only within this brief but critical period
of time during Steinbeck's development as a writer that
Lawrence's fiction provided a model for Steinbeck; and, even
though Steinbeck's reading of Lawrence greatly influenced the
ritual as well as the psychological nature of the works of
this period, the study of the Lawrence-Steinbeck relationship
needs to be further qualified by the apparent limited amount
of Lawrence's fiction actually read by Steinbeck.

Lisca does not pursue the implications of his statement on Lawrence and Steinbeck, but he does immediately
follow his statement on Steinbeck's psychological interests
by noting that "Elisa Allen in 'The Chrysanthemums, ' Mary
Teller in 'The White Quail, ' Amy Hawkins in 'Johnny Bear, '
and the anonymous woman in 'The Snake' are psychological
portraits of frustrated females. "[3] Even though Lisca's
juxtaposition provides little information for the task of de-
termining the extent of Lawrence's influence on To A God
Unknown and its great emphasis on male activity, it does
provide an area of consideration that, when united with other
Lawrencean themes more directly concerned with To A God
Unknown, narrows the search for specific works of Lawrence
read by Steinbeck to a definite period of development in
Lawrence's career.

67

The idea of the frustrated female initially establishes
a general connection between several of the stories in The
Long Valley and the fiction of Lawrence that extends back to
Lettie in The White Peacock and encompasses most of Lawrence's major works. This sense of female frustration,
particularly for Lawrence, is sexual and it is usually mani-
fested by the female through a denial of her own sexuality
and her conscious attempt to possess the male by undermin-
ing his natural position of authority in the male-female relationship. In Steinbeck's "The White Quail" Mary Teller's
willful denial of the real world and her acceptance of the
artificial world of her trim and ordered garden in its place
reveals her own lack of female vitality, but the effect that
her obsession with the garden has on her husband, Harry,
is to deny his manhood, indirectly revealed in her contempt
for his business practices, so that her girlhood dream can
be realized and preserved. She retains her innocence (spirit) but, at the same time, isolates and devitalizes Harry's
maleness. She functions, in relation to the male, in somewhat the same fashion as Mrs. Morel, in Sons and Lovers,
who usurps the male role of authority in the family and, in
the process, denies the maleness in her husband and prevents her sons from having fulfilling relationships with wom-
en other than herself. Despite the symbolic impact of Harry's killing of the white quail, his sense of complete loneliness and desolation at the end of the story marks his fate
as similar to that of Anton Skrebensky in The Rainbow and
Gerald Crich in Women in Love, two men victimized by the
female who withholds her essential self from the male and,
at the same time, sucks away his male vitality.

Though the Lawrencean woman who insists on denying
her natural female role of submission usually responds de-
structively towards her male partner, Lawrence did not completely fault the female figure in the breakdown of the male-
female relationship. He believed that the woman assumed
the unnatural position of dominance because modern man had
lost the sexual potency to keep her in a submissive role.
Anton Skrebensky is destroyed as a male by Ursula Erang-
wen's withdrawal from him, but her rejection of the man is
necessitated by his failure to respond completely to Ursula's
need to be fulfilled as natural woman (universal being) rather
than Ursula (personal being). In other words, Ursula wants
to lose her identity with the world, all the "old dead things, "
and be restored to her natural place in the cosmos. Rather
than seeing himself as the center of the universe and the female as a vital yet subordinate part of the cosmos, this

type of Lawrence male has a love for dead and mechanical
things that immobilizes him to the extent that, as he builds
his world, he fails to realize his own male uniqueness; and,
to fill the void created, he turns back to the female for
comfort, security, and even his identity. [4]

The failure of the male to define himself in natural
relationship with the female and to provide the source of
power for the female figures is treated prominently in the
stories in The Long Valley which deal directly with the
plight of the male. In "The Harness" Peter Randall's
trapped condition extends beyond the grave, as his dead
wife retains her domination of his life. Jim Moore, in "The
Murder," must learn to reach the deep passionate nature of
his wife or accept the prospect of repeated instances of cuck-
oldry. The final condition for the male who refuses to
assert his natural male authority is isolation and loneliness.
Jim's act of violence is the proper response to the dark
side of his wife, and it restores him to his natural position
as dominant male. Harry Teller can destroy the symbol of
his wife's spirituality, but in the real world his condition
remains the same: "'What a dirty skunk, to kill a thing she
loves so much.' He dropped his head and looked at the
floor. 'I'm lonely,' he said. 'Oh, Lord, I'm so lonely!'"[5]

The despair that comes from the deterioration of the
male-female relationship is most revealingly presented in the
condition of one of the frustrated females of The Long Valley.
Eliza Allen, of "The Chrysanthemums," is a woman of great
vitality, but her sense of being alive, of being in vital contact with nature, is not confirmed by the male world. Her
husband, Henry, does not function importantly in the major
encounter of the story, but Steinbeck reveals Henry's insen-
sitivity to the female through his male activities and his
conversation with Eliza. Henry sees the world through male
eyes and, in turn, recognizes only the male's capacity for
passion; he is shocked by Eliza's interest in prize fights,
and, when previously faced with the physical presence of an
aroused rather than usually placid wife, he responds by telling her that she looks "so nice."

Eliza's attraction to the wandering tinker is a mani-
festation of her desire for the freedom of the male, but, at
the same time, her fascination for his way of life is evoked
by images that suggest it is her female sexuality that needs
to be set free:

'I've never lived as you do, but I know what you
mean. When the night is dark--why, the stars
are sharp-pointed, and there's quiet. Why, you
rise up and up! Every pointed star gets driven
into your body. It's like that. Hot and sharp
and--lovely' [p. 18].

When she finds her gift, the chrysanthemums, lying along
the road, she recognizes again the treachery of the male,
the willingness of the male to exploit her naturalness for
profit or comfort. Her interest in the prize fights, like
her desire for the wine, is a desperate attempt to retain
the passion aroused by her encounter with the tinker. When
her husband suggests that she will not enjoy the fights, she
accepts the wine as a substitute; but her sense of female defeat and her loss of sexual potency is overpowering: "She
turned up her coat collar so he could not see that she was
crying weakly--like an old woman" (p. 23).

The period of Lawrence's most violent reaction to the
deterioration of the male-female relationship, what H. M.
Daleski terms as Lawrence's "One Up, One Down" period,
is particularly relevant to the relationship between Lawrence
and Steinbeck. What distinguishes this period from others
in which Lawrence was also concerned with this basic relationship is the development of a leadership theme. At this
time, Lawrence also emphasized characters who, according
to Daleski,

> are to be concerned with 'advance and increase, '
> that they are to be 'projected into a region of
> greater abstraction, ' of 'pure thought and abstract-
> ed instrumentality, ' in their journey 'into the un-
> known'; in terms of Lawrence's attribution of male
> and female qualities, that is to say, they are to
> be engaged in characteristic male activity. 6

This period of male dominance in Lawrence's fiction
invites a comparison between the new hero of Lawrence and
Steinbeck's natural leader, Joseph Wayne, of To A God Unknown. The novels written by Lawrence during this period
develop the idea of a natural leader, who maintains power
through his intimate contact with the cosmos and his ability
to translate that concept into a myth that revitalizes the
souls of the people. Lawrence begins, in Aaron's Rod with
the dilemma of Aaron Sissoa, who through the guidance of
his friend, Rawdon Lilly, discovers the necessity for the re-

establishment of male friendship and male activity in the
world as a means to nurture the male sexual potency back
to a condition of health and power. In Kangaroo and The
Plumed Serpent, Aaron's discovery is transmitted into male
action. The relationship between Richard Somers, the Lawrence figure in Kangaroo, and Ben Cooley or Kangaroo, the
leader of the Diggers, a secret military organization, is a
study of the potential for the assertion of male power in the
world of politics. When Somers rejects Kangaroo and his
world of political activity, he does so on the grounds that
Kangaroo's form of male activity is restricted to the work-
ings of the mind or spirit. It forces the lower self to respond to the dictates of the mind-will and, in the process,
destroys the vital, passionate part of man. Somers' response to the dying Kangaroo anticipates The Plumed Serpent
and sounds the note of comparison between Don Ramon of
The Plumed Serpent and Steinbeck's Joseph Wayne:

> The only thing one can stick to is one's own iso-
> lated being, and the God in whom it is rooted.
> And the only thing to look to is the God who ful-
> fills one from the dark. And the only thing to
> wait for is for men to find their aloneness and
> their God in the darkness. [7]

Both Don Ramon and Joseph Wayne are actualizations
of the heroic male described by Richard Somers. Both
characters find their "aloneness," which is their sense of
individual contact with the surrounding universe; and both
find the "God in the darkness" which is the rediscovery of
their intimate connection with the mystery of the cosmos.
Don Ramon expresses this idea of the God-man through his
attempt to revitalize the old Mexican God, Quetzalcoatl. The
importance of this god figure for Don Ramon is that he represents the entire span of life; he is "lord of both ways."
Don Ramon rejects Christianity as a natural religion for man
because it appeals strictly to the spirit and must be understood consciously to have an effect. What man needs is not
a god of the mind, but rather a god who encompasses spirit
and soul, both the above and the below. In Quetzalcoatl, the
Plumed Serpent, Don Ramon has found a symbol of heaven
(Quetzal-bird) and earth (Coatl-serpent).

Don Ramon's part in restoring Quetzalcoatl to man
is that of First Man of Quetzalcoatl. In this role, Don Ramon becomes one of the Initiators of the Earth. He further
describes himself as one of the natural aristocrats of the

world, a man who is defined and prevented from merging
with other aristocrats by his race, but, nevertheless, a man
who is set apart from the common mass of his race by his
intense awareness of complete physical being. He wants
Mexicans to learn the name, language, and rituals of Quetzalcoatl so that they may also speak in their own blood consciousness. The revival of the old gods of Mexico by their
new prophet, however, is a more conscious attempt to appre-
hend and bring into harmony the basic duality of existence.
This abstract event is most completely actualized in the marriage of Kate and Cipriano performed to the primitive rhythm
of ancient ceremony, consummated by the coming of the rain,
the perfect expression in nature of the unity of above and below.

        Steinbeck's Joseph Wayne has the potential to be a
priest of the people. After his last meeting with Joseph,
Father Angelo is shaken by "the force of the man." His
thoughts capture the "threat" to the church posed by Joseph
and, at the same time, offer a striking parallel between the
natures of Don Ramon and Joseph Wayne: "'Thank God this
man has no message. Thank God he has no will to be remembered, to be believed in.' And in sudden heresy, 'else
there might be a new Christ here in the West.'"[8] Joseph,
like Don Ramon, is a member of the natural aristocracy of
man. He possesses the same phallic power of a Don Ramon,
and he, too, feels confirmed in that power by his sense of
being one with the universe (his desire for the land) and his
acceptance of the heritage of the race (the traditional blessing from his father). Once Joseph arrives at Nuestra
Señora, the long valley of our lady, he becomes aware of
the coming together of his biological and racial heritage,
"for his father and the new land were one" (p. 5). Though
Joseph's god is unknown, the power that he senses in the
universe becomes polarized in the figure of the father. He
consigns his father's spirit to a giant oak tree; thus, again,
he unites spirit and nature in the same way that Don Ramon
does through the image of Quetzalcoatl. What remains for
Joseph is to summon his brothers to settle in the valley, and
for Joseph, himself, to enter into the rhythm of life by
marrying and giving his seed to a woman capable of receiv-
ing it.

        In both The Plumed Serpent and To A God Unknown,
the power of the god is distilled in the man. As Rama, wife
of Joseph's brother, Thomas, explains,

'I tell you this man is not a man, unless he is all
men. The strength, the resistance, the long and
stumbling thinking of all men, and all the joy and
suffering, too, cancelling each other out and yet
remaining in the contents. He is all these, a re-
pository for a little piece of each man's soul, and
more than that, a symbol of the earth's soul'
[p. 66].

If Don Ramon becomes sometimes too formal and even dull,
it is because he is attempting to articulate a godliness that
has its source in the blood consciousness of man. He faces
the task of formulating a Lawrencean philosophical position
in the language of a primitive religion and people. Yet he
remains in complete control of his own sense of being and
preserves that sense of aloneness and detachment Lawrence
believes would lead to the "God in the darkness."

Joseph Wayne's sense of power is more closely
aligned with his unconscious urges, since he rarely attempts
to articulate his primitive awareness of the God-in-the-man. [9]
Because of this, his natural religion, his tree and rock worship, seems more a part of the man than Don Ramon's religion of Quetzalcoatl. The situation Joseph Wayne encounters also eventually becomes entirely different from that
faced by Don Ramon. Once Joseph's brother, Burton, gir-
dles his father's tree, Joseph is faced with a crisis of the
land rather than of the people. When the following winter
comes, it brings no rain with it. The baptismal act of
nature that announces the rebirth, growth, and unity of all
living things is now denied Joseph Wayne and the land. His
role of King-god, the god-like man who dominates and
breathes his life into the land, is drastically changed. He
now becomes the Fisher King and must bear a new responsibility for the now dying land. According to Joseph Fontenrose, "Joseph is a Frazerian divine king who must die
because he has lost his divine potency."[10]

Joseph's shift from King-god to Fisher King marks
an important distinction between the heroes of To A God Unknown and The Plumed Serpent. It also suggests the likelihood that, despite the basic similarities between the two
characters in their awareness of their complete physical
being and their intimate connection with the cosmos, Steinbeck may not have borrowed directly from The Plumed Serpent. A more probable source of influence, one that offers
the possibility of sacrifice as a means for restoring the

natural order of things but still supports the concept of the
natural, heroic man presented by Lawrence in The Plumed
Serpent, is a collection of short stories entitled, The Woman
Who Rode Away. [11] Three stories in the collection, "Sun,"
"The Woman Who Rode Away," and "The Man Who Loved
Islands," seem particularly related to the completion of
Steinbeck's To A God Unknown. Added to this possibility
of a direct influence, moreover, is the further possibility
that several stories in the Lawrence collection which are
studies of frustrated, sexless females may have influenced
the creation of those equally frustrated females who appear
in those stories in The Long Valley previously mentioned.

Even though the main characters of "Sun" and "The
Woman Who Rode Away" are females, the stories are comparative with To A God Unknown in imagery and theme.
"Sun" is the story of Juliet, a bored and tired American
woman who is brought back into intimate connection with the
natural world through her worship of the powers of the sun.
As she lies naked on a rocky bluff of a Mediterranean island
and absorbs the rays of the sun, she is restored to a new
and vital sense of femaleness. Though the story is united
thematically with To A God Unknown in its stress on the
close relationship between man and the cosmos, what is of
particular importance for the Lawrence-Steinbeck relationship is the similarity between the phallic scenery of "Sun"
and that of To A God Unknown. In both works, the power
of nature to penetrate the human soul is presented in sexual
terms. When Juliet bathes naked in the sun, she can feel
it penetrate her body. The sun pulsates its warmth "even
into her bones, even into her emotions and thoughts."[12]
At the place where she bathes she notices "one cypress
tree, with a pallid, thick trunk, and a tip that leaned over,
flexible, up in the blue. It stood like a guardian looking to
sea; or a low, silvery candle whose huge flame was darkness against light: earth sending up her proud tongue of
gloom" (p. 25). The idea of Juliet coming under the power
of phallos is even further suggested by a fertility ritual in
which she wanders naked in the gully between the two estates
and encounters the vital, dark-faced peasant whose passion
and seed she desires but cannot have because of her husband's return from the mechanical and hostile world she now
dreads.

Similarly, Joseph Wayne's feelings for the land are
closely related to sexual urgings. He senses a "curious femaleness" about the land, and when his possessiveness of

the land becomes a passion he responds in a way that in-
verts the passive acceptance of Juliet:

> He stamped his feet into the soft earth. Then the
> exultance grew to be a sharp pain of desire that
> ran through his body in a hot river. He flung
> himself face downward on the grass and pressed
> his cheek against the wet stems. His fingers
> gripped the wet grass and tore it out, and gripped
> again. His thighs beat heavily on the earth [p. 8].

After his violent embrace, Joseph is left tired and frightened
by his "moment of passion," but, as he rests that evening,
the act is presented again to him in phallic scenery similar
to that viewed by Juliet as she lies naked in the sun:

> After a while the honey-colored moon arose behind
> the eastern ridge. Before it was clear of the hills,
> the golden face looked through bars of pine-trunks.
> Then for a moment a black sharp pine tree pierced
> the moon and was withdrawn as the moon arose
> [p. 8].

Even Juliet's passage along the gully and its suggestiveness
of a fertility rite is similarly evoked in Joseph's entry
through the pass with his bride, Elizabeth. According to
Joseph Fontenrose, the event is

> fertility ritual and a rite de passage, complete
> with scapegoat sacrifice. For Benjamin was killed
> at this time while engaged in the sex act, repre-
> senting the mock king who was killed to insure the
> safety of the real king; and the killer was not pun-
> ished but vanished for a time like the killers of
> the sacred ox in Athens. 13

"The Woman Who Rode Away" and "The Man Who
Loved Islands" have a more thematic relationship with To A
God Unknown. If the two Lawrence stories are examined together, they present a study of the scapegoat king whose
death is required for the refertilization of the land. "The
Man Who Loved Islands" tells about a man who isolates himself from humanity by moving from island to smaller island
until he is left alone at the mercy of the destructive elements. The similarity between this Lawrencean hero and
Joseph Wayne exists in the attitude of the people toward their
acknowledged leader and the way in which each man negates

the possibility of human contact as he becomes increasingly
obsessed with a barren, dying world. The hero of Lawrence's story is called "the Master" by those who are initially allowed to share the island as his servants. One of the
women, the farm-wife, also recognizes qualities in him that
"made you think of Our Saviour Himself" (p. 207). Similarly, when Elizabeth, at her wedding, tries to imagine the figure of Christ, she creates "the face, the youthful beard, the
piercing puzzled eyes of Joseph, who stood beside her" (p.
47). On other occasions, both Father Angelo and Juanito
recognize the Christ in Joseph, but whereas Father Angelo
sees the power of Christ in the man, Juanito recognizes the
defeated, crucified Christ.

     The difference between "the Master" and Joseph
Wayne lies in the nature and significance of their deaths.
Lawrence's hero is driven into isolation more by his dread
of intimate human contact and his fear of betrayal than by
his need to restore his natural relationship with the cosmos.
His destruction during the snow and cold of winter parallels
the mindless death of Gerald Crich in Women in Love. His
death, unlike that of Joseph Wayne, offers no hope for the
restoration of life. As he dies he imagines himself in the
midst of summer; but the illusion quickly fades and he becomes aware again of the approaching snow. Joseph Wayne's
eventual isolation is more of an indication of his own need
to accept total responsibility for the dying land. Any sacrifice, human or animal, proves irrelevant as the universe
seems to await the death of the King-god himself. Accordingly, as the life flows out of the veins of Joseph's slashed
wrists, he becomes aware of the growing darkness and the
approaching rain. The moment, however, is not illusory;
as Joseph dies "the storm thickened, and covered the world
with darkness, and with the rush of waters" (p. 179).

     The idea of human sacrifice as the means of restor-
ing the harmony between man and the land is explored by
Lawrence in "The Woman Who Rode Away." In this story,
one of Lawrence's bored American women goes on a quest
to find a mysterious tribe descended from the Aztecs.
When she wanders upon the tribe they take her, almost
with her consent, as a human sacrifice. What is important
in this story beyond the depiction of the death-will of the
white woman is the reason the Indians want the woman as a
blood sacrifice. They feel her voluntary coming is a sign
that their mystic contact with the cosmos, denied them by
the domination of the land by the whites, is to be restored.

In other words, her death will herald the re-establishment
of the living connection between their people and the land.

The general relationship between "The Woman Who
Rode Away" and To A God Unknown is the Fisher King
theme. This similarity, by itself, raises no serious question of influence since the writings of J. G. Frazer and
Jessie Weston were familiar to both writers. Yet when the
similarity is added to those between "Sun, " "The Man Who
Loved Islands" and To A God Unknown, the evidence of possible influence increases. Of particular importance in directly comparing "The Woman Who Rode Away" and To A
God Unknown are the presentations of the death scenes of
the major characters. Lawrence's "girl from Berkeley" is
carried on a litter through a valley covered with snow. The
bearers enter a group of pinetrees and follow the stream
bed of a now dry stream until they come to a wall of solid
rock. Behind a huge, inverted pinnacle of ice, naked priests
are waiting in a cave for her arrival. The woman is
stripped of her native garments and taken into the cave for
the blood sacrifice. She is laid on a large flat stone as the
priests with their knives wait for the death moment, which
will come when the sun completely fills the cave.

Though Joseph Wayne takes his own life (the woman
in Lawrence's story never resists her fate), several similarities are apparent in the cause of the deaths of the two
characters. Joseph sacrifices himself for the same reason
that the Indians take the white woman's life. Just as the
Indian priests await the sun as the signal to slay their victim and reassert their natural heritage of the sun and the
moon, Joseph slashes his wrists to avow his oneness with the
land. As blood gushes from his wrists the elements respond
accordingly. As Joseph loses consciousness of his body,
the needed rain begins to fall. Almost at the moment of
death, Joseph articulates the connection between man and
the cosmos sought through the blood sacrifice: "'I am the
land,' he said 'and I am the rain. The grass will grow out
of me in a little while'" (p. 26).

The sacrificial settings are also similar in the two
works. The rock or mountain, as the heart of the land,
functions as the place of sacrifice; and, in each story, the
rock-mountain contains a cave and provides the source for
a now dried-up stream. It is also completely surrounded
by pine trees. In each setting, the cave is central to the
significance of the death of the main character. In "The

Woman Who Rode Away" the cave becomes the place of execution, but, because of the intent of the act, it actually becomes the place where the redemption of the people begins.
Joseph Wayne dies while lying atop the rock, yet as the
blood flows from his wrists onto the rock, it becomes obvious
that he now provides the life stream that previously flowed
from the cave.   From out of the cave previously came the
life flow, the hope for man; but that flow has now become
the blood of man and woman.   The cave now seems to sym-
bolize the darkness in the human soul which contains the
God in man, for it is man's own blood that restores him to
his proper place in the mystery of the cosmos.

          Certain stories in The Woman Who Rode Away which
directly approach the problem of the male-female relationship offer further parallels between Lawrence and Steinbeck
and increase the likelihood of an influence. [14] Domineering
females and their dominated or defiant male partners frequently provide the subject matter for stories in both The
Woman Who Rode Away and The Long Valley. Of the frustrated, sexless females who appear in the Lawrence stories,
those in "Two Blue Birds" and "None of That" are particularly similar to the Steinbeck women in "The White Quail"
and "The Snake. " "Two Blue Birds" is Lawrence's rather
lightly satirical treatment of a sexless love triangle between
two females and a male.   The struggle for control over the
male is waged between his wife and his secretary.   The
wife attempts to conquer her rival by forcing her will in
opposition to the husband and the secretary, while the secretary prefers to gain control over the male by assuming the
passive role of complete obedience.   Of particular importance
in comparing "Two Blue Birds" with "The White Quail" is
Lawrence's use of bird imagery to define the character of
the female.   Lawrence accentuates the lack of sexual vitality
in the struggle of the two females by presenting the parallel
skirmish of two blue birds.   The similarity between the ineffectual fight between the blue birds and the insignificant
clash of words between the two females is brought home
rather forcibly when the two human combatants face each
other while dressed in blue.

          In "The White Quail" Mary Teller's lack of sexual
vitality is revealed by Mary herself, when she identifies
with the rare white quail which drinks at the pool in her
garden. Her appeal to her husband, Harry, to kill the
prowling cat further indicates her fear of any physical contact with the world outside her garden. She denies the

world outside the jurisdiction of her will. Harry's dilemma
is that he, too, is dominated by the female. His decision
to kill the quail rather than the cat symbolizes a brief assertion of his maleness, but, at the end of the story, his fate
remains that of the sexually vigorous male who, because of
the female's dominance, acknowledges and accepts the conditions of isolation and despair.

Ethel Cane in "None of That" and the mysterious
woman in "The Snake" are two other females unwilling to
participate physically in a male world. They are comparative on a much more ominous basis than Mary Teller and
Lawrence's "two blue birds." The woman in "The Snake"
gratifies vicariously her obsession to dominate and identify
with the male; she watches her newly acquired possession,
a male rattlesnake, methodically kill and devour a laboratory
rat. During the experience the woman identifies with the
snake, the victimizer. She desires the male role denied to
her by her own nature. She cannot participate in her natural
role with the male, so she is forced to own and admire the
male power she cannot cope with as a woman.

Ethel Cane, of "None of That," also refuses the female role; she wants "none of that" physical contact with the
male. Her admiration for Cuestra, the matador, parallels
the fascination of Steinbeck's strange female for the rattlesnake. Ethel also has a fantastic desire to possess, to assert her female will and power upon the male world. She
claims, moreover, that her desire is for the world of imagination not the physical male world. In Cuestra's performance in the bullring she witnesses brutalized life idealized into an art form. Just as Steinbeck's woman identifies
with the ritual of the snake's performance, Ethel responds
to the quick, cruel movements of the matador, her "beast
with an imagination." Yet what she really admires in Cuestra's performance is a deadliness that counteracts Hemingway's aesthetics of the bullring, and instead brings the fictional worlds of Lawrence and Steinbeck together again in
theme and imagery. When Ethel says that she sees a "marvelous thing" in Cuestra, her male companion and escort
replies "But so has a rattlesnake a marvelous thing in him:
two things, one in his mouth one in his tail. But I didn't
want to get a response out of a rattlesnake" (p. 299). Dr.
Phillips, in "The Snake," makes the inverse comparison by
suggesting that "it's better than a bullfight if you look at it
one way, and it's simply a snake eating his dinner if you
look at it another" (p. 80).

The conclusions of the two stories are presented dif-
ferently. Ethel is raped by a bullfight gang after she is in-
vited to Cuestra's house. Later, she commits suicide to
preserve her imaginative vision of an idealized world. Steinbeck's snake lover simply disappears, and is never seen
again by Dr. Phillips. Yet, though the events are not parallel, the effect of the endings is quite similar. In both cases,
the female is presented as an unnatural being. Her end signifies her refusal or inability to exist or survive as a woman in the real world.

The sexually frustrated female and the male-god as-
serting his oneness with the mystery of the cosmos offer
striking counterparts for the male-female relationship. For
Lawrence, they represent individuals who are very much a
part of a world that is based upon the interaction of the
male and the female. The extremes they represent are in-
dicative of the perpetual struggle of both sexes for dominance
and the destructive potential in a war of wills. Appropriate-
ly, in Lawrence's final period of writing, exemplified by
Lady Chatterley's Lover, there is again an appeal for reconciliation, for a way in which man and woman can preserve
their separate identities but still engage in an intimate sexual and imaginative union.

The frustrated female, the King-god, is more unusual
in Steinbeck's world. In much of Steinbeck's fiction after
the period which includes To A God Unknown and The Long
Valley the female often provides the source of strength for
the faltering male. The male, on the other hand, is presented more and more as part of the group organism, a man
no greater than the function he performs in relation to his
social or political group. The period in which the fictional
worlds of Lawrence and Steinbeck come together is brief,
but the contact spawns some of the strongest and strangest
characters in Steinbeck's fiction. More importantly, it allowed Steinbeck to pursue an important area of human feelings and responsiveness. His eventual movement away from
a world so intensely personal in its psychological and sexual
orientation to one more social and moral in content is less
the artist's retreat as it is a recognition of the nature of
his artistic sensibilities.

Notes

1. Harry Thornton Moore, The Novels of John Steinbeck

and D. H. Lawrence   81

(Chicago: Normandie House, 1939), p. 92.

2. The Wide World of John Steinbeck (New Brunswick, New
    Jersey: Rutgers University Press, 1958), p. 95.

3. Ibid.

4. Gerald Crich of Women in Love and Sir Clifford Chat-
    terley of Lady Chatterley's Lover are the most
    striking examples of the Lawrencean male who is
    unable to respond to the passionate side of life and
    is forced to seek the comfort of the maternal figure.

5. The Long Valley (New York: Viking Press, 1938), p.
    42. All subsequent quotations will be taken from
    this edition.

6. The Forked Flame: A Study of D. H. Lawrence
    (Evanston, Illinois: Northwestern University Press,
    1965), p. 189.

7. Kangaroo (New York: Viking Press, 1963), p. 335.

8. To A God Unknown (New York: Bantam Books, 1968),
    p. 172.

9. I refer you again to Father Angelo's comment on Jo-
    seph Wayne's potential power as a religious leader
    of the people.

10. John Steinbeck: An Introduction and Interpretation (New
     York: Holt, Rinehart, and Winston, 1963), p. 16.

11. I am indebted to Bobby L. Smith, a Lawrence scholar
     and admirer of Steinbeck, for suggesting The Woman
     Who Rode Away as the probable source of Lawrence's
     influence on Steinbeck. The stories were published
     in America in 1928.

12. The Woman Who Rode Away (New York: Alfred A.
     Knopf, 1930), p. 26.

13. Fontenrose, p. 16.

14. No story in The Woman Who Rode Away parallels the
     stories of youth in The Long Valley. There are,
     however, some similarities between Lawrence's

"The Prussian Officer," a story appearing in an
earlier collection, and "Flight." Both stories present in vivid and brutal terms the ordeal of escape
and death for the young man who has committed
murder. "The Vigilante," in its equation of the
experience of the lynching mob and the sex act,
also seems under the influence of Lawrence, but
I have not been able to trace the story to a specific
source. "The Leader of the People" is indebted
more to Steinbeck's developing ideas on the group
man than Lawrence's concept of the leader.

6. STEINBECK AND DANIEL MAINWARING

Steinbeck and Mainwaring: Two Californians for the Earth
by Richard Astro

Perhaps more than in any other decade in the twentieth century, the 1930's witnessed the emergence of a host of writers espousing various political and social doctrines in hundreds of essays, novels, and short stories.   Every conceivable ideology, from Naziism to Communism to social agrarianism had its literary spokesmen, whose books, because of their propagandistic formats, are now dated and forgotten.

In sorting through the vast literary melange of the thirties, now and then one discovers a writer whose works have been too hastily discarded; a man whose writings are not dated propaganda, but are both critically important for the light they bring to bear on the work of his more famous contemporaries and are intrinsically valuable as good literature.   One such writer is a Californian named Daniel Mainwaring, author of an important novel, One Against the Earth (1933) and an excellent short story, "Fruit Tramp" (1934), both of which are of significant value in a study examining themes and structures in Steinbeck's California writings. Moreover, while "Fruit Tramp" is a period piece, though certainly a well-written one, One Against the Earth is a highly significant novel which, as this study will show, deserves re-discovery and reprinting. 1

"Fruit Tramp, " published in Harper's in 1934, is a well-plotted and deftly-styled piece about a migratory labor dispute in the Elberta peach orchards near Fresno, California.   Called by Mainwaring "a forerunner to the Steinbeck book (In Dubious Battle), "2 it views the plight of the migrants through the sympathetic eyes of a small farmer who sees the migrants not as "Rooshian" conspirators, but simply as "pitiful and white-faced" people who do not have enough food to eat.

In this story, published before either <u>In Dubious Bat-</u>
<u>tle</u> (1936) or <u>The Grapes of Wrath</u> (1939), there are several
stylistic and thematic elements typically associated with
Steinbeck's political novels.   First, Mainwaring demonstrates
a sensitivity towards the California landscape, and such passages as

> It was hot that year.   There had been little rain
> and when June came the mountain tops were bare
> of snow.   From the valley you could see little
> patches near the ragged crest of the ridge, like
> bits of paper scattered through the trees.   The
> canals were dry and the river was so low we didn't
> dare go swimming because they said we'd get ty-
> phoid fever. 3

recall Steinbeck's unique descriptive talents in so many of
his California novels.   Moreover, Mainwaring's portrait of
the small farmer, caught between the migrants' struggles
and the impersonal operation of the large land corporations
reminds one of the dilemma faced by the small farmer
named Anderson in <u>In Dubious Battle</u> and by the small farmer who hires Tom and Pa Joad near the Weedpatch camp in
<u>The Grapes of Wrath.</u>   Similarly, Mainwaring's description
of the way in which the mortgage companies foreclosed upon
the small landowners after World War I,

> The mortgage companies came, took the Lincolns
> and Cadillacs out of the barns, loaded the furniture
> the farmers had bought in good times into moving
> vans and drove away, and the banks foreclosed on
> the land and took over some of the farms [235].

looks forward to one of Steinbeck's memorable portraits of
the machines in the Oklahoma gardens in <u>The Grapes of</u>
<u>Wrath:</u>

> The tractors came over the roads and into the
> fields, great crawlers moving like insects, having
> the incredible strength of insects.   They crawled
> over the ground, laying the track and rolling on it
> and picking it up. ...   Snub-nosed monsters, rais-
> ing the dust and sticking their snouts into it,
> straight down the country, across the country,
> through the fences, through dooryards, in and out
> of gullies in straight lines. ...   The tractor cut a
> straight line on, and the air and the ground vi-

> brated with its thunder.   The tenant man stared
> after it, his rifle in his hand.   His wife was be-
> side him, and the quiet children behind.   And all
> of them stared after the tractor. [4]

Finally, Mainwaring's depiction of the quiet, yet over-
poweringly strong unnamed migrant leader, "a big man with
broad shoulders, " through whose shirt one could see "mus-
cles on his arms like big lumps" (238), instantly suggests
Steinbeck's character of London in In Dubious Battle whom
the novelist describes as "a large man" with "immense
shoulders" and "thick dark hair" whose "face was corded
with muscular wrinkles and his dark eyes were as fierce
and red as those of a gorilla. "[5]   And the conclusion of
"Fruit Tramp, " in which the big man is killed,

> A gun went off and a red flame pointed at the big
> man.   He puts his hands over his belly and started
> moving backward, very slowly, toward the grove,
> but he didn't get there.   Maybe he tripped over
> something, I don't know; but he fell down and a
> woman came running out to him, took his head in
> her arms, and started to cry [242].

is similar to the climactic scene in Steinbeck's novel in
which Jim is felled by an assassin's bullet:

> There was a roar, and two big holes of light.
> Mac had sprawled full length.   He heard several
> sets of running footsteps.   He looked toward Jim,
> but the flashes still burned on his retinas.   Gradu-
> ally he made Jim out.   He was on his knees, his
> head down....   Mac put out his hand to lift the
> head [249].

In actuality, similarities in style and plotting aside,
too much should not be made of the thematic parallels between "Fruit Tramp" and Steinbeck's political novels.   Both
men, having personally witnessed the migrants' plight, were
dealing with virtually the same fictional materials.   More
importantly, Mainwaring and Steinbeck's common attitude toward the California agricultural dilemma was widespread
among western liberals during the thirties.

Nevertheless, while the most that can be said about
the similarities between "Fruit Tramp" and Steinbeck's political novels is that they exist and deserve to be acknowl-

edged, the parallels between the two writers become more
substantial when one turns to Mainwaring's longer fictional
work, One Against the Earth.

Published by Smith and Long of New York in January
of 1933, One Against the Earth is a somber novel which
chronicles the life story of Eugene Hamus. Born and raised
on a small ranch in California's San Joaquin Valley, Eugene,
who nourishes an obsessive passion for adventure in far off
places, escapes a possessive mother and a loveless marriage
and wanders through the midwest and southwest, first as a
newspaper reporter covering the daily Los Angeles police
blotter, and then as an apprentice to a religious fanatic,
pasting religious slogans on barn walls and billboards. Finally driven home after being acquitted of having murdered
a woman he picked up during the course of his wanderings,
Eugene, while warmly received by his mother, is reviled by
his old friends who look for and ultimately find an opportunity to lynch him.

In one sense, the novel, as Lisle Bell pointed out almost as soon as the book appeared, has more momentum
than depth. [6] The characters, excluding Eugene, are never
sufficiently rounded, hampering Mainwaring's attempt to en-
liven and vitalize his central thematic thesis. But despite
these deficiencies, to which may be added the rather clumsy
plotting of the novel's almost Dreiserian determinism, the
author's occasional lapsing into sentimentality and the book's
generally episodic structure, One Against the Earth is an
honest novel that portrays the novelist's genuine knowledge
of and feeling for California's lands and its people. As
Mainwaring himself has told this writer, while "Earth isn't
a very good book, it does have the feel of the valley and
the farm people. "[7]

One Against the Earth abounds with lyrical and highly
moving pictures of the California landscape, written by a
man profoundly sensitive to his fictional materials:

> Spring came from behind the mountains bringing
> swift color to the cheeks of hills. With it came
> rain, softening the crust upon the earth and start-
> ing the sap in the vines and trees. The bare
> fields of the Hamus ranch became green overnight
> as the alfalfa sprouted and the tender leaves pushed
> themselves toward the sun....

> Tarweeds came up again, their velvet leaves pos-
> sessing a sharp, clean smell. And in the bottom
> of the ditches rushes grew and the frogs came out
> and began their singing. All about was life. In-
> side the clods, worms moved blindly, burrowing
> forward. Gophers nibbled on the roots of plants,
> throwing up piles of fine earth as they went
> along....
>
> The fields were alive. There was the scent of
> poppies, of filaree, of fiddle-necks, of mustard.
> There was the heavy scent of earth, the bitter
> smell of new alfalfa, the salt smell of sweaty
> horses, the rich odor of manure. [8]

Green fields, the scene of poppies and alfalfa, nibbling
gophers and singing frogs--this is Steinbeck language which
could find a place in any of a dozen of the Californian's
novels. In fact, the general thrust of the above passages,
summarized in Mainwaring's remark that "all about was life"
and that "the fields were alive" captures the essence of
Steinbeck's ecologically conceived descriptions of nature in
which, as the novelist wrote in the Sea of Cortez, "Everything is everywhere. "

Thematically, as well as descriptively, there are
many similarities between Mainwaring's view of the land in
One Against the Earth and those expressed by Steinbeck.
These parallels are qualified, however, by one central difference. For while nearly all of Steinbeck's protagonists
love the land, not only for its beauty but also for its ability
to provide man with meaning in life, Mainwaring's leading
character, Eugene Hamus, regards it as a menacing force
which fetters him and inhibits his personal self-emancipation.
Indeed, the main action of Mainwaring's narrative describes
Eugene's vain attempts to free himself from the earth and
his ultimate recognition that he really belongs on the soil.

> About him lay his fields; trees planted by his own
> hand, throwing their shadows on the clods. The
> endless croaking of the frogs seemed the earth's
> song of triumph at this man's capture. He was
> trapped in the net of stars, a prisoner of the soil
> [84].

To counter Eugene's hostility towards the earth, Mainwaring creates in Eugene's mother an earth-mother figure

who, like Steinbeck's Rama Wayne in To A God Unknown and
Ma Joad in The Grapes of Wrath, seeks to keep her family
intact by holding her son close to the soil.   Realizing her
son's desire for adventure ["Here was a boy filled with wanderlust who must be tethered to the earth, who must be
made to feel a love for a simple, ordered life" (34)], Mary
Hamus struggles in vain to keep Eugene on the ranch.   And
late in the novel, when Eugene discovers how his mother
"once felt my first faint struggles and trembled with an unknown fear, " when "I was strong, tearing at her, trying to
leave my warm home" (270), he wonders, watching her go
about her daily chores, "if she is immortal like the earth.
Is she the earth--old mother earth?" (270) And Mary, seeing her son after so many years, realizes (in language pat-
ently loaded with earth imagery) that her son has finally
come home:

> Seed of my lover, earth of my body, mingling in
> the storehouse of my belly until this plant forsook
> its mother plant to tower beside it, a new, differ-
> ent growth, yet yearning for the old tree still.
> Two trees of the same species beside the relic of
> their past that brought them to this bit of land be-
> neath their feet [271].

     Perhaps the place in One Against the Earth where
Mainwaring most nearly approaches Steinbeck's view of nature occurs when the novelist states his belief that man is
inherently related to the land; that, when viewed properly,
the family of man blends with the soil and is "an integral
part of the earth. "

> They were alone in the doorway with a brown field
> that merged into the green of pines and the gray of
> brush before them. So quietly they stood, they
> too blended with the soil. Man, woman, cabin
> seemed an integral part of the earth. ...
>
> Ed's voice sounded dimly in the distant scene:
> 'This is ours. We are a part of it. '
> 'For how long?'
> 'Forever, ' his voice said [11-12].

One has only to recall Joseph Wayne's remarks to his wife
in To A God Unknown, Casy's speeches to Tom Joad about
man's relationship with the land in The Grapes of Wrath,
and Sam Hamilton's statement to Adam Trask about his love

for his "dust heap" in <u>East of Eden</u> to note Steinbeck's iden-
tical belief in man's kinship with the soil.

Similarly, when Mainwaring describes a farmer named
Harbin, a tall and muscular man whose

> face was kind and full of peace, gained through
> long association with the soil and its plants and
> animals, and who is content to live here always
> with his daughter, seeing few men, hearing the
> bleating of his sheep, the lowing of his cattle, for
> music [112-113].

the reader knows he is encountering the type of contented individual Steinbeck's Joads so desperately wanted to become
in <u>The Grapes of Wrath.</u>

Mainwaring, like Steinbeck, creates characters in his
novel who mock and are wholly insensitive to the agrarian
ideal.   In particular, one notes the religious fanatic, Isaiah,
for whom Eugene works writing what Isaiah has entitled "The
Book of Death. "   Isaiah, who scoffs at those who till the
earth, insists to his protégé that he was right to run away
from home since "farmers are all fools, that's why they stay
on the soil" (103).   In this connection, one remembers the
overly pious Burton Wayne, whose disgust for Joseph's feeling for the land forces him to leave the Wayne ranch and go
to live in a religious camp in Pacific Grove.

After his sojourn with Isaiah and with a host of other
people who block his return to the land, Eugene, finally returning home after his acquittal, realizes that he simply
wants to be "left alone with the sky and the earth"; that,
in fact,

> there was nothing better than this, the soft night
> of the valley, the cold stars.   All the ambition
> was gone from him; he wanted to love, to work
> and to sleep--to see the moonlight filter through
> the trees, to taste the clean smell of earth thrown
> up by the plow, to hear the soft pounding of en-
> gines [299].

His return completed, Eugene suddenly understands that his
identification with nature is complete.   For sitting alone in
the darkness, "he became part of the earth.   Against the
night his body took on a rugged beauty that blended with the

gnarled trunks of the peach tree" (299).

Ironically, like so many Steinbeck characters (particularly in The Pastures of Heaven) who come to understand their relationships with nature only to have them quickly dashed to pieces by the hostile world of men, Eugene's identification with the land is short-lived, for almost immediately following his moment of self-realization, he is accosted by his neighbors and lynched for a crime he did not commit. What is important in this instance, however, is that Eugene finally recognized his kinship with the land, even though he was not allotted the time to enjoy it.

In addition to Mainwaring's descriptive talents in depicting the California landscape and its people, and his thematically crucial ritualistic devotion to the earth, both of which are central in so many of Steinbeck's writings, there is one further element in One Against the Earth which possesses a distinctly Steinbeckian flavor. For as Eugene passes through the United States, meeting all kinds of people while painting Isaiah's religious slogans on rocks and fences and on the walls of barns and sheds, he concludes that Americans, despite their poverty and wretchedness, are basically kind and openhearted--a feeling which leads to his positive faith in mankind:

> As he drove he developed a theory, new to him, about man; saw him in the light of his experiences, pictured him as a gigantic blunderer, stumbling toward some goal, foolish perhaps, but for the most part kind and good. Blinded by ignorance, held down by poverty, and in the face of it, sometimes happy, ready to help his fellow man.
>
> This was America. It was a symphony, tones blending until the resultant harmony was great. Men worked in California. Men worked in New York. Men were statues against the furnace flame. Men were figures of earth. Everywhere there was life, humans groping for light.
>
> On the hill, he was strong and the earth was his. These men laboring beneath him, cutting down the forests, tearing up the soil, building, tearing down, rebuilding, loving, fighting, begetting children, dying--they were all his. They were strong men. Disease, yes, --and death. But for the most part

life was a glorious thing. Men were kind. Universal brotherhood and love [161-162].

The chanting optimism of these lines resembles so many similar passages in Steinbeck's work that further explanation hardly seems necessary. One only has to recall Steinbeck's definition of "manself" (in The Grapes of Wrath) who "reaches, stumbles forward, painfully sometimes"; who, "having stepped forward, may slip back, but only half a step, never the full step back," and who continues to "grow beyond his work" and "emerge ahead of his accomplishments" (204, 205), and his final affirmation in America and Americans that "we have failed sometimes, taken wrong paths, paused for renewal, filled our bellies and licked our wounds; but we have never slipped back--never,"[9] to note his enduring belief in America.

It is, of course, impossible to assess Steinbeck's debt to Mainwaring, if indeed any debt exists at all. Conversely, it is even possible that Mainwaring drew on the early Steinbeck, though One Against the Earth was published shortly after Cup of Gold and before any of Steinbeck's major works. On the other hand, it is a well-known fact that Steinbeck was an indiscriminate borrower. Indeed, as Jack Calvin, a personal friend of Steinbeck and co-author with Ed Ricketts of Between Pacific Tides, has told this writer, "John borrowed from other people too, using and misusing his friends."[10] Thus Steinbeck seems to have depended in his writing on the ideas of others (particularly on those of Ricketts).

Moreover, that Steinbeck knew Mainwaring and One Against the Earth has been substantiated by Mainwaring himself who, in a recent letter to this writer, recalls that they met in 1933 at U. C. L. A.

The head of the English department had us out to speak to his small class of budding writers--introduced us as two young Californians who would make their mark in the literary world. He was fifty percent right. (Steinbeck had just published Cup of Gold, I, Earth.)[11]

So, while any evidence of a connection between Mainwaring and Steinbeck is at best circumstantial, the many similarities between the writers' feeling for the earth combined with the substantial knowledge that they knew each other early in Steinbeck's career, suggests at least the possibility of such a connection. Viewed properly, however, the most important thing about Mainwaring's work in relation to Steinbeck's writing is that, irrespective of any direct relationships between the two men, Mainwaring's feeling for the earth and for the people seems to heighten the reality of California novels. In short, "Fruit Tramp" and <u>One Against the Earth</u> make Steinbeck's Salinas Valley a little more real; and the reader, having examined Mainwaring's attitude towards the land and its power to direct the course of human existence, sees Steinbeck's similar reverence for the earth as more comprehensible and believable, if somewhat less unique.

Notes

1. There is very little biographical information about Mainwaring. The following account is by the writer himself: "I was born in Oakland because there were no hospitals in Dunlap, California--on the edge of Sequoia National Park. Mother's family were San Franciscans. Her brother was one of Hearst's right hand men on the <u>Examiner</u>. My old man came over from England in 1888, took one look at the Sierras and said that's where he was going to spend out his days. He did. Through Gifford Pinchot he got a job at the top of the forest service in California when it was started. He worked his way to the bottom. We lived in Dunlap, Weaverville, San Luis Obispo and finally North Fork in 1910. In 1911 the old man bought twenty acres in Clovis thirteen miles out of Fresno and moved his rather large family down there. We planted it to grapes and peaches. I worked as a peach picker and grape picker in the twenties and rubbed elbows with Wobblies. Been a pseudo-anarchist ever since. Worked on newspapers, in motion pictures publicity. Wrote a flock of mediocre mystery novels and finally turned to screen writing which I'm pretty good at." Mainwaring goes on to point out that at the present he is writing a screen play for a crime novel entitled <u>Silver Street</u> by E. Richard Johnson.

2. Daniel Mainwaring, in a letter written to Joel Hedgpeth of the Marine Science Center, Newport, Oregon, April 27, 1969.

3.   Daniel Mainwaring, "Fruit Tramp," Harpers, 169
     (July, 1934), 236. All further citations from "Fruit
     Tramp" refer to this edition and are identified by
     page number in the text.

4.   John Steinbeck, The Grapes of Wrath, Compass Books
     edition (New York, 1958), pp. 47, 53. All further
     citations from The Grapes of Wrath refer to this edi-
     tion and are identified by page number in the text.

5.   John Steinbeck, In Dubious Battle, Bantam Books edition
     (New York, 1961), p. 38. All further citations from
     In Dubious Battle refer to this edition and are iden-
     tified by page number in the text.

6.   Lisle Bell, New York Times Review of Books, January
     29, 1933, p. 8.

7.   Daniel Mainwaring, in a letter to Richard Astro, June
     1, 1969.

8.   Daniel Mainwaring, One Against the Earth (New York,
     1933), pp. 29, 56. All further citations from One
     Against the Earth refer to this edition and are iden-
     tified by page number in the text.

9.   John Steinbeck, America and Americans (New York,
     1966), p. 205.

10. Jack Calvin, in a letter to Richard Astro, July 14, 1969.

11. Daniel Mainwaring, in a letter to Richard Astro, June 1,
     1969.

7. STEINBECK AND JOHN MILTON

Steinbeck's <u>East of Eden</u> and Milton's <u>Paradise Lost</u>: A
Discussion of "Timshel"
by John L. Gribben

When John Steinbeck began to write <u>East of Eden,</u> he
felt that he was about to undertake the most impressive en-
deavor of his career. As he envisioned the novel, it was
to embrace a "philosophy old and yet new born;"[1] it was to
relate "one of the greatest, perhaps the greatest story of
all--the story of good and evil, of strength and weakness, of
love and hate, of beauty and ugliness. "[2] In the story itself,
Lee, the Chinese philosopher-servant, stated a rule--"a
great and lasting story is about everyone or it will not last"[3]
--and that rule followed Lee's judgment that "no story has
power, nor will it last, unless we feel in ourselves that it
is true and true of us" (268). To carry the burden of this
"philosophy old and yet new born, " and to universalize a tale
that should be "true and true of us, " Steinbeck chose "the
powerful, profound and perplexing story in Genesis of Cain
and Abel" as one which, with its implications, "has made a
deeper mark on people than any other save possibly the story
of the Tree of Life and original sin. "[4]

Steinbeck uses the basic Cain and Abel narrative of
Genesis 4:2-16, to explain the freedom of all men to do or
to avoid evil. For Steinbeck the crucial word in the text is
<u>timshel,</u> the Hebrew word which occurs in the Lord's ex-
planation to Cain of why he should not be angry at the Lord's
rejection of his sacrifice:

> And the Lord said unto Cain, 'Why art thou wroth?
> and why is thy countenance fallen? If thou doest
> well, shalt thou not be accepted? and if thou doest
> not well, sin lieth at the door. And unto thee
> shall be his desire, and thou shalt rule over him'
> [Gen. 4:6-7].

Lee explains the significance of the words "thou shalt":

> The American standard translation 'Do thou' orders
> men to triumph over sin, and you can call sin ig-
> norance. The King James translation makes a
> promise in 'Thou shalt,' meaning that men will
> surely triumph over sin. But the Hebrew word,
> the word timshel--'Thou mayest'--that gives a
> choice. It might be the most important word in
> the world. That says the way is open. That
> throws it right back on a man. For if 'Thou may-
> est'--it is also true that 'Thou mayest not.' Don't
> you see? [303].

In the Journal of a Novel: The East of Eden Letters
Steinbeck insists upon the importance of his exegesis. "May,"
he writes, "is a curious word in English. In the negative
it is an order, but in the positive it allows a choice. Thou
mayest not is definite but thou mayest implies either way--
do you see?"[5] Lee interprets this idea further:

> Any writing which has influenced the thinking and
> the lives of innumerable people is important. Now,
> there are many millions in their sects and churches
> who feel the order, 'Do thou,' and throw their
> weight into obedience. And there are millions
> more who feel predestination in 'Thou shalt.'
> Nothing they may do can interfere with what will
> be. But 'Thou mayest'! Why, that makes a man
> great, that gives him stature with the gods, for
> in his weakness and his filth and his murder of
> his brother he still has the great choice. He can
> choose his course and fight it through and win
> [303].

The word timshel--thou mayest--is for Steinbeck,
then a charter issued by God declaring men to be free. As
the thesis develops, Steinbeck's timshel concept grows until
it includes not only the declaration of man's freedom to
choose between doing good or evil, but, as Joseph Wood
Krutch suggests, a further implication that man is not "the
victim of his heredity, his environment, or of anything
else."[6] Oppressed by Aaron's goodness, Caleb, with a
feeling of being rejected, and a strong sense of the evil
that is in him, repudiates the idea that his mother's wicked-
ness is part of his own:

Cal said, 'I was afraid I had you in me. '
'You have, ' said Kate.
'No, I haven't. I'm my own. I don't have to be
you. '
'How do you know that?' she demanded.
'I just know. It just came to me whole. If I'm
mean, it's my own mean' [466].

Lee had affirmed the same concept when Cal, heartbroken at
the notion, suggested that he understood his mother "because
I've got her in me. " Lee admits that Cal has "that" in
him. Everybody has, but,
'You've got the other too. Listen to me! You
wouldn't even be wondering if you didn't have it.
Don't you dare take the lazy way. It's too easy
to excuse yourself because of your ancestry. Don't
let me catch you doing it! Now--look close at me
so you will remember. Whatever you do, it will
be you who do it--not your mother' [449].

Cal's mother was a whore, and Abra's father a thief,
but, with timsel, both Cal and Abra make their own desti-
nies, despite their blood. Lee, again, sums it up:

'I thought that once an angry and disgusted God
poured molten fire from a crucible to destroy or
to purify his little handiwork of mud. I thought
I had inherited both the scars of the fire and the
impurities which make the fire necessary--all inherited, I thought. May be you'll come to know
that every man in every generation is refired....'
[600].

The stricken Adam's final timshel is more than a blessing
and a forgiveness for Cal. It is a reminder that even after
Cal's weakness and his filth and his murder of his brother,
he still has the great choice which gives him stature with
the gods. He can still choose his course and fight it
through and win.

In Paradise Lost Milton asserted the same freedom
for man, illustrating his thesis with another basic story, the
story of Adam and Eve and their fall. Theology in Milton's
day had muddied the issue of human freedom, balancing the
freedom of man against the foreknowledge of God, and finding man to be not so free as he had thought he was. Milton's prime concern was to justify God's ways to man, but

much of his justification involved establishing the man whose
mind God "hinder'd not Satan to attempt" as a man "with
strength entire, and free will armed."[7]

      Milton establishes man as free, not only despite the
foreknowledge of God, but even in the face of what might be
considered a decree foretelling his fall.   In Book III of the
epic God, cognizant of Satan's approach to the earthly paradise, is aware, too, that Satan plans by force or guile to
pervert man, God's new creation, "...and shall pervert
(III, 91).   "Shall" can be used to express determination,
command, promise, or prophecy; "will" would express simple expectation.   This does not seem to leave man much
hope, whether it expresses a command to Satan, or a prophecy concerning mankind.   Yet God continues, stressing
man's freedom despite the "shall":

> For Man will heark'n to his glozing lies,
> And easily transgress the sole Command,
> Sole pledge of his obedience: So will fall
> Hee and his faithless Progeny: whose fault?
> Whose but his own? ingrate, he had of mee
> All he could have; I made him just and right,
> Sufficient to have stood, though free to fall
> [III, 92-98].

The "will" of "so will fall" (l. 94) may imply simple expectation, but nothing can destroy the absolute fact of man's
freedom as proclaimed by Milton's God.   Such freedom was
a necessary condition in man, according to Milton's reasoning:

> What pleasure I from such obedience paid,
> When Will and Reason (Reason also is choice)
> Useless and vain, of freedom both despoil'd,
> Made passive both, had served necessity,
> Not mee [III, 106-111].

That Adam is free to do good or evil is evident further,
from the warning to be conveyed to Adam by Raphael:

> ... advise him of his happy state,
> Happiness in his power left free to will,
> Left to his own free Will, his Will though free,
> Yet mutable;... [V, 234-237].

When Adam insists that he is bound to the will of God
because of God's goodness in creating him, and because of
the happiness Adam is experiencing through that goodness,
Raphael stresses the fact that moral obligation imposes no
necessity on man's will:

> ... That thou art happy, owe to God;
> That thou continu'st such, owe to thyself,
> That is, to thy obedience; therein stand.
> This was that caution giv'n thee; be advised.
> God made thee perfet, not immutable;
> And good he made thee, but to persevere
> He left it in thy power, ordain'd thy will
> By nature free, not over-ruled by Fate
> Inextricable, or strict necessity;
> Our voluntary service he requires,
> Not our necessitated, such with him
> Finds no acceptance, nor can find, for how
> Can hearts, not free, be tri'd whether they serve
> Willing or no, who will but what they must
> By Destiny, and can no other choose? [V, 520-534].

Adam himself has learned well the lesson of his freedom.
When Eve argues that their happiness in Eden is frail, and
that Eden is no Eden because of the threat of Satan, Adam
answers that God has ordered all things perfectly and has
given to man everything necessary to secure his happy state
from outward force.   However,

> ... within himself
> The danger lies, yet lies within his power:
> Against his will he can receive no harm.
> But God left free the Will, for what obeys
> Reason, is free, and Reason he made right, ...
> [IX, 347-351].

While it is obvious that Adam and Eve could not claim
to be victims of environment or heredity, Milton does consider the objection that the freedom of choice in our first
parents was impaired because of the fore-ordaining knowledge
of God.   God Himself deals with that point:

> They therefore as to right belong'd,
> So were created, nor can justly accuse
> Thir maker, or thir making, or thir Fate;
> As if Predestination over-rul'd
> Thir will, despos'd by absolute Decree

> Or high foreknowledge; they themselves decreed
> Thir own revolt, not I: if I foreknew
> Foreknowledge had no influence on their fault,
> Which had no less prov'd certain unforeknown
> [III, 111-119].

Thus John Milton and John Steinbeck, each in his own time and in his own way, affirmed the doctrine of man's free will, and the responsibility of every man to stand accountable for his own actions in choosing between right and wrong, good and evil. It would be rash to claim a Miltonic influence on Steinbeck's work, although at least once before Steinbeck had played a Miltonic theme. In an earlier novel, In Dubious Battle (1936), Steinbeck not only took his title from Paradise Lost (I, 104), but he portrayed a character who could be read as possessing many characteristics of Milton's Satan. 8 However, it is possible to draw parallels without involving unwarranted conclusions, and there are similarities as well as differences in Paradise Lost and East of Eden. Both are epic in scope and in intent. Milton returns to the origins of mankind and probes the cosmic depths and heights. Steinbeck, "using the Biblical story as a measure of ourselves,"9 extends his story to envelop three generations of Trasks and to cover the length and breadth of the United States. Both Steinbeck and Milton use biblical material and both works are essentially scriptural in inspiration. That both centered on the freedom of man's will is interesting, but the problem has always attracted thinkers as a "philosophy old and yet new born. " Milton treats the problem in the context of his time, establishing men as free in the face of an alleged divine determination. Steinbeck, in reaction against a current philosophy which binds man to do as blood or circumstances direct him, insists that man is free to act, to liberate himself from his past and conquer evil.

There are differences. Milton's epic is an attempt to justify the ways of God to man. Steinbeck is more interested in justifying the ways of man to men and of each individual to himself. Milton asserts eternal providence. Lee, speaking of the timshel concept, insists, "This is not theology. I have no bent toward gods. But I have a new love for that glittering instrument, the human soul. It is a lovely and unique thing in the universe. It is always attacked and never destroyed--because 'Thou mayest'" (304). Steinbeck is concerned with man's freedom to fulfill himself, and such fulfillment is impossible unless man has freedom of choice

in doing good or evil. Milton's ultimate consideration is
man's role in creation to fulfill all things in Christ, as is
obvious from the last books of his epic. Steinbeck is occu-
pied with good and evil, only superficially with sin as Milton
would have understood it, and with no trace of "supernal
Grace contending / With sinfulness of Men" (XI, 359-360).
Milton's God is scarcely acknowledged in the Steinbeck thesis.
When Samuel asks Lee, "Do you then not think this is a divine book written by the inky finger of God?", Lee answers,
"I think the mind that could think this story was a curiously
divine mind. We have had a few such minds in China too"
(302).

    Both Milton and Steinbeck encounter difficulties in
their enunciation of the timshel concept. For Steinbeck the
problem would involve the goodness of Adam and Aaron who,
apparently incapable of being anything but good, serve as
foils to the meanness of Charles and Caleb. Cathy, intrigu-
ing as she is, is created a monster, and she cannot help
being what she is. Timshel seems not to apply to Cathy nor
to Adam and Aaron; Adam's brother, Charles, is never directly examined in the light of the timshel doctrine. Only
Cal is immediately subject to the onus of a choice, and he
could very well have gone the way of Charles if it were not
for Lee's sometimes startling insistence on timshel. "Yes,
I believe it, and you had better believe it or I'll break every
bone in your body," Lee says to Cal at one point (449). Yet,
despite the characters of Adam Trask and Aaron, and even
Cathy, Steinbeck's thesis comes through with clarity as well
as with insistence. He is concerned, not with goodness, or
even with evil, but with freedom.

    Milton's plight is even more intense, since he is in
many ways incapable of explaining away the actual insufficiency
of Adam and Eve to stand in the face of temptation. In Paradise Lost he avoids the endless wandering mazes of the infernal speculation on "Providence, Foreknowledge, Will, and
Fate, / Fixt Fate, Free will, Foreknowledge absolute" (II,
559-560), although he does explain his concepts of predestina-
tion and the divine decrees at some length in his treatise on
The Christian Doctrine. Milton's critics have, however, aug-
mented his poetry with explanations designed to clarify what
Milton took for granted in his epic. Christopher Ricks poses
the essential question--"if they could fall, were they not in
some sense already fallen?"[10]--and Stanley E. Fish provides
the essential answer--

Actually the opposite is true: if they could not
fall, they could not stand; that is, <u>they</u> would not
be doing the standing, consciously and willingly.
The ability not to fall depends on the ability to fall;
free will is a meaningless concept unless the possibility of wrong choice exists. [11]

That, essentially, is the doctrine of <u>timshel.</u>

Writing of <u>Genesis</u> and <u>Exodus</u>, Helen Gardner suggests that these books, rejected as history, "have returned
as myths valued for their symbolic meaning as expressive
of the human predicament and the divine response to it."[12]
She calls them "divinely inspired fictions, by which the truth
of things is shadowed to the imagination and intellect."[13]
If ever all other measures fail or are discarded, this could
be the ultimate rule whereby the greatness of Milton's <u>Para-</u>
<u>dise Lost</u> will find its lasting measure, that it used these
"divinely inspired fictions" to portray the human condition
and to offer it consolation. Similarly, whatever else can be
said of the success or failure of John Steinbeck's <u>East of</u>
<u>Eden</u>, it is surely "a passionately moral declaration of Stein-
beck's vision of the human condition."[14] It is also his affirmation that man will endure.

"'Thou mayest rule over sin,'" Lee. That's it. I
do not believe all men are destroyed. I can name
you a dozen who were not, and They are the ones
the world lives by. It is true of the spirit as it
is true of battles--only the winners are remembered. Surely most men are destroyed, but there
are others who like pillars of fire guide frightened
men through the darkness. "Thou mayest, Thou
mayest!" What glory!' [308-309].

That Milton and Steinbeck were artists is beyond
doubt, and there is no question here of the superiority of
one over the other. That both wrote literature is equally
beyond doubt, although whether the literature they wrote was
not at the same time a species of tract is debatable. We
may call Steinbeck's philosophic tenets "thematic patterns"
if we wish, but they participate in the nature of propaganda,
just as Milton's declared justification of the ways of God to
man was propaganda, the complexity of which is still not
fully explored. For Steinbeck, perhaps, passionate affirmation was far more effective for his thesis than it might have
been for Milton, since Steinbeck, confronting a very negative

and defeatist generation, was fighting a far more dubious battle than Milton, who had much more liberty to please as well
as to teach.   Much of Milton criticism centers on Milton as
a thinker, and most of Steinbeck criticism concerns itself
with what he says rather than with how he says it.

          Nonetheless, both men were artists, as has been
said, and a comparison of their ideas might reasonably involve a comparison, or at least an evaluation, of the two
men as artists.   Milton's art is obviously the more secure
of the two.   There is little necessity for convincing in the
projection of his own convictions.   Milton is able to stand
detached in his artistic efforts to justify the ways of God to
man in a theocratic universe, since he can celebrate, almost without question, man's choice in accordance with man's
right reason, and concern himself with rational man free to
serve or not to serve.   On the other hand, Steinbeck, writing
for a time that has stripped man of much of his traditional
humanity, must exert all of his artistry to clothe man with
at least a semblance of the dignity which he once owned.
Passionately moral declaration must be part of his art, and
Steinbeck declares himself effectively without hawking his
thesis, without a maudlin evangelism which might, by sheer
insistence, enervate what it was intended to vitalize.

          Through his art Milton encouraged man to feel that,
although freely fallen, he may freely rise, through God's
grace.   Steinbeck uses his art to insist, effectively, that
whatever the worldly-wise might say to inure man in his
fallen state, man can, because of timshel, rise in the ruins
of the universe which he has pulled down upon himself.

          The rest is academic.   The quality of Milton's epic is
conserved by Milton's explanation of what he conceived an
epic to be.   The faults of execution are obvious, although
those faults do not affect what Milton has wrought as a substantial thing.   It can be maintained that Steinbeck's East of
Eden, as variously and as severely as it has been criticized
as a novel, has justified itself because it has accomplished
what it set out to do.   It has told a story and it has told it
well.   It has maintained its pace and its mood, through imagery and language, through character and incident, and it has
touched upon, even insisted upon, a basic human problem for
which it has provided a basic humanistic solution.   If his
generation and subsequent generations squirm at Steinbeck's
thesis and reject it, it is only because he insisted upon it
too late, and to critics who have long lost sympathy with

what he endeavored to say.   Milton, it might be added, has
suffered the same rejection.

Notes

1. John Steinbeck, Journal of a Novel: The East of Eden
    Letters (New York: Viking Press, 1969), p. 3.

2. Ibid. , p. 4.

3. East of Eden (New York: Viking Press, 1952), p. 270.
    Subsequent citations are from this edition and appear
    in the text.

4. Steinbeck, Journal of a Novel, p. 90.

5. Ibid. , p. 120.

6. Joseph Wood Krutch, "John Steinbeck's Dramatic Tale of
    Three Generations, " New York Herald Tribune Book
    Review, 21 September, 1955.   Cited in Steinbeck and
    His Critics, ed. E. W. Tedlock, Jr. and C. V. Wick-
    er (Albuquerque, New Mexico: University of New
    Mexico Press, 1957), p. 304.

7. John Milton, Paradise Lost, Book X, 11. 7-8.   Subse-
    quent citations from Paradise Lost will be identified
    in the body of this article.   The text used is John
    Milton Complete Poems and Major Prose, ed. Mer-
    ritt Y. Hughes (New York: The Odyssey Press, 1957).

8. Mac is a vicious exponent of Machiavellian opportunism,
    a supporter of lost causes, a leader of the dispos-
    sessed.   Lester Jay Marks suggests, in Thematic De-
    sign In the Novels of John Steinbeck (The Hague:
    Mouton Press, 1969), p. 18, that "we may marvel
    at Mac's devotion to his cause, and at his power, but
    we despise his brutal means to dubious ends. "   War-
    ren French, in John Steinbeck (New York: Twayne
    Publishers, Inc. , 1961), p. 83, cites In Dubious Bat-
    tle as a portrayal of "the manipulation of people's
    dreams for selfish purposes. "   In many ways Milton
    could not have described his Satan more accurately.

9. Steinbeck, Journal of a Novel, p. 105.

10. Christopher Ricks, <u>Milton's Grand Style</u> (New York:
       Oxford University Press, 1963), p. 99.

11. Stanley E. Fish, <u>Surprised by Sin: The Reader in
       Paradise Lost</u> (New York: St. Martin's Press, 1967),
       p. 210.

12. Helen Gardner, <u>A Reading of Paradise Lost</u> (Oxford:
       The University Press, 1965), p. 10.

13. <u>Ibid.</u>, p. 22.

14. Marks, <u>Thematic Design in the Novels of John Stein-
       beck</u>, p. 131.

8.   STEINBECK AND J. D. SALINGER

Steinbeck and Salinger: Messiah-Moulders for a Sick Society
by Warren French

John Steinbeck and J. D. Salinger share the distinction of having produced--little more than a decade apart--
two of the very few novels to have been enthusiastically received by both public and critics.   The Grapes of Wrath
(1939) and The Catcher in the Rye (1951) were both high on
best-seller lists for many months; and, although both novels
were coolly received by genteel intellectual critics, they received high praise from sensitive readers. 1   Except for possibly Sinclair Lewis's Main Street (1920), what other American novels have been so received?   In a country where popular and critical tastes are often irreconcilable, the achievement of the two novels is remarkable.

Because the ambiences of the novels are very different, however, they have rarely been compared.   Steinbeck's
novel is the apogee of the "underdog" literary tradition of
the 1930's.   It deals--like Faulkner's As I Lay Dying (1930)--
with a group of rural people who cannot even be dubbed "proletarian, " because they exist precariously entirely outside
the bounds of organized society.   Many polite readers doubt-
less shared the sentiments of the California service-station
helper who says, "Them goddam Okies got no sense and no
feeling. "

The Catcher in the Rye, on the other hand, crafted
quite consciously in the F. Scott Fitzgerald tradition, deals
with one of the most privileged urban groups in these United
States--the residents of the Central Park section of New
York City who can send their children to expensive prepara-
tory schools.   The characters in the two novels are clustered
around the extreme opposite ends of the American social
spectrum (and neither author in any work successfully dealt
with the other's specialty); yet perhaps these two extremes
should be viewed not as the ends of a continuum but as near-

ly the same point on a circle--the extremely overprivileged
share common discontents.

Certainly the novels are stylistically similar. Both
rely heavily upon a kind of colloquial language that squeam-
ish readers find offensive. Both, I argue, have served to
provide one of those perennially essential refurbishings of
the American literary idiom that breaks the hold of the dead
hand of the past upon it and brings it closer to expressing
the feelings of the discomforted elements in American society.

Yet even here there is a significant difference between
the novels. The Grapes of Wrath employs the unconsciously
substandard language of a group that never had the privilege
of learning what gentlewomen-schoolmarms with what Emily
Dickinson called "dimity convictions" forced upon their cap-
tive audiences as "standard English." Steinbeck's characters
are people who wish desperately to be accepted by the society that rejects them. "We're Joads," Ma says, "We
don't look up to nobody." She complains that the policeman
in Needles, California, made her feel "ashamed," but she is
relieved that in the Weedpatch government camp she feels
"like people again." She and the family enter enthusiastically into the business of setting up a government and trying to
shed the stigma of poverty by disappearing into the general
society.

The Catcher in the Rye employs, on the other hand,
the self-conscious sub-standard language of a defiant boy
who rejects "standard English" as one of the hallmarks of
the successful "phonies" that he despises. Holden Caulfield
wants to get out of the society that the Joads strive to get
into. "We'll stay in these cabin camps and stuff like that,"
Holden proposes to an unenthusiastic girl friend, "till the
dough runs out. Then ... I could get a job somewhere and
we could live somewhere with a brook and all .... I could
chop all our own wood in the wintertime." He elects the
very life that the Joads reject (except for the oldest son,
Noah, who leaves the family to live by "a nice river," but
Steinbeck shows his distaste for Noah's solution by allowing
the character simply to disappear from the narrative).

The Joads and Holden do share the pastoral ideal that
is the basis of the vanishing Jeffersonian dream. When the
Joads are forced off their tenant farm in Oklahoma, they do
not think about migrating to the big city and going on relief
(after Rosasharn's husband does leave the family in hopes of

getting a technical job in town, Steinbeck dismisses him
from the fable as he had earlier Noah). The family dreams
instead of going to California and making a fresh start as
farmers in an idyllic setting. "We had hard times here."
Pa Joad says, "'Course it'll be all different out there--
plenty work, an' ever'thing nice an' green, an' little white
houses an' oranges growin' aroun'." Salinger's boy, on the
contrary, dreams that he will finally go West in order to
pose as a deaf-mute, "meet this beautiful girl that was also
a deaf-mute" and marry. "If we had any children, we'd
hide them somewhere."

Contrastingly public and private as these visions are,
both blossom from the American myth of the perpetual fron-
tier, although Holden's later vision is even more primitivis-
tic than the Joads', reaching wistfully back to before the day
that Stephen Crane brought the bride to Yellow Sky. Both
the Joads and Holden hope to retreat to an earlier America,
that is almost surely purely mythical. Both writers, therefore, in what seem indisputably their major works, take on
the role of artist as magician, conjuring up out of the "foul
dust" of American disillusionment colloquial Messiahs.

Both exhibited at contrasting points in their career,
an unhealthy interest in manufacturing Messiahs. Very early
Steinbeck barely managed to get published what remains his
most hermetic work, To A God Unknown (1933), in which Joseph Wayne accepts the regeneration of society as his calling
by committing suicide on a mysterious boulder and proclaim-
ing as he dies, "I am the land, ... and I am the rain. The
grass will grow out of me in a little while." Earlier a conventional Roman Catholic priest has said of Joseph, "Thank
God this man has no message. Thank God he has no will to
be remembered, to be believed in ... else there might be a
new Christ here in the West."

Very late in his productive career, Salinger published
his most hermetic work, the short story "Teddy," in which
the title character--a boy of ten--predicts the day of his
mysterious death and goes to it unprotestingly because he
feels that he is not "believed in." Earlier he has said,

> 'I was six when I saw that everything was God, and
> my hair stood up, and all that.... My sister ...
> was drinking her milk, and all of a sudden I saw
> that she was God and the milk was God. I mean,
> all she was doing was pouring God into God, if

you know what I mean. '

American readers have found both Joseph Wayne and
Teddy pretty far out (curiously, in contrast, the characters
in Steinbeck's last novel The Winter of Our Discontent and
Salinger's first published story "The Young Folks" (1940) are
almost equally preciously banal), but in the mid-career figures of Jim Casy and Seymour Glass both writers succeeded
in striking a balance between their personal visions of the
"oneness" of all creation and the popular taste of a society
composed of individuals frightened at venturing beyond the
egocentric security of their own skins.

I don't think--because of the different directions in
which the artists were moving--any talk of "influence" is at
all relevant.   What forces the comparison is both men's demand at the high point of their careers for the spiritualiza-
tion of our increasingly materialistic and meretricious society.   I can account for Steinbeck's decreasing spirituality
and Salinger's increasing spirituality as they aged only by
suggesting that Steinbeck, beginning his career during a period of depression, found solace in the increasing material rewards that came from his efforts, whereas Salinger, beginning his career during a period of affluence, became increasingly distrustful of the solace of material rewards.
Perhaps what both men suggest is that an artist at the
height of his powers must be in opposition to the prevailing
temper of his times, whatever that temper!

Certainly the major works of both men are--despite
the failure of critics following the lead of John W. Aldridge's
In Search Of Heresy (New York, 1956, pp. 129-131) to perceive their structures[2]-- records of not just physical but
spiritual odysseys.   Both the Joads and Holden Caulfield
were originally socially rejected because of their own care-
lessness--the Joads ruined the natural cover of their land by
overplanting; Holden lost the fencing equipment that has great
symbolic value to a school that must continually battle to
maintain its competitive status.   Both the Joads and Holden
also embark upon impractical quests.   The dream home of
the Joads is already in the possession of people who will
fight desperately to retain it; Holden is at least compelled
to admit, "You can't ever find a place that's nice and peaceful, because there isn't any. "

Both the Joads and Holden are also originally motivated by basically selfish drives.   Although the Joads' concern

is for the "fambly" and Holden's for little children, both en-
vision the group that they consider their responsibility as at
odds with society generally.   In one of the most famous passages in The Grapes of Wrath, Ma Joad defies Pa when he
talks of breaking the family into groups to expedite the ex-
pedition to California: "All we got is the fambly unbroke.
Like a bunch of cows when the lobos are ranging, stick all
together.   I ain't scared while we're all here, all that's
alive, but I ain't gonna see us bust up. "

        In perhaps the most famous passage in The Catcher
in the Rye, Holden tells his little sister Phoebe,

> 'I keep picturing all these little kids playing some
> game in this big field of rye and all.   Thousands
> of little kids, and nobody's around--nobody big, I
> mean--except me, and I'm standing on the edge of
> some crazy cliff.   What I have to do, I have to
> catch everybody if they start to go over the cliff--
> I mean if they're running and they don't look where
> they're going. '

Ma Joad's warning about cows when the lobos are ranging
applies very well to Holden's vision of innocence and the fall.

        Yet both of these very moving concepts are naively
impractical in a mobile society, since both demand a patri-
archal order that can flourish only in a scantily populated and
highly fertile area. 3   In megapolis, families do break up
and cute little children must grow up into "phonies. "

        The function of our mass media today seems to be to
delude viewers into believing that while these family break-
ups will happen to everyone else, they can't happen to them.
What distinguishes Steinbeck's and Salinger's novels from
this sentimental claptrap--versions of television soap opera--
is that both authors do insist that people must accept conscious responsibility for decisions that they make.   Neither
The Grapes of Wrath nor The Catcher in the Rye are static
magic-lantern slides of sentimental disaffiliation from the
present to enjoy a communion with a hallucinatory past.
Both the Joads and Holden are shaken out of their trance-
like "exclusiveness" into a sense of communality.

        When the residents of the boxcar camp described in
the last chapters of The Grapes of Wrath pool their efforts
to fight a common threat, Ma Joad observes, "Use' ta be

the fambly was fust. It ain't so now. It's anybody. Worse
off we get, the more we got to do." She has come at last
to share--and to be able to express in her own words--
preacher Casy's vision in the early chapters of the book.
"Maybe all men got one big soul ever-body's a part of."
Tom Joad has come to share this vision, for when his mother is worried that she may not know what has happened to
him, he tells her that if Casy is right it doesn't matter,
"Then I'll be all aroun' in the dark. I'll be ever'where--
wherever you look.... If Casy knowed, why, I'll be in the
way guys yell when they're mad an'--I'll be in the way kids
laugh when they're hungry an' they know supper's ready."

Holden realizes, too, that he must give up his dreams
of protecting children from growing up. Watching his sister
ride a carrousel in Central Park, he reports with anguish,

> 'All the kids kept trying to grab for the gold ring,
> and so was old Phoebe, and I was sort of afraid
> she'd fall off the goddam horse, but I didn't say
> anything or do anything. The thing with kids is,
> if they want to grab for the gold ring, you have
> to let them do it, and not say anything. If they
> fall off, they fall off, but it's bad if you say any-
> thing to them. '

That this recognition of the impracticality of his earlier elit-
ist vision has led him to a sense of communality is shown
by his concluding remarks in the novel, "About all I know
is, I sort of miss everybody I told about."

These characters approach their new senses of communality with vastly different feelings. Although the Joads'
position remains extremely precarious, their discovery of
communality is a triumph that allows Rosasharn to share her
most intimate possession--the breast-milk intended for her
dead baby--with a dying old man. For Holden, on the other
hand, although he is assured of the best of care at home and
at the sanatorium where he is recovering, the acceptance of
"everybody" is a defeat, the destruction of the most beautiful dream that he will ever know.

But we must remember that the Joads started out
seeking acceptance, whereas Holden sought disaffiliation.
Their feelings upon discovering a brotherhood of men are
bound to differ sharply, though both novels do depict characters who had once sought to isolate themselves but who

and J. D. Salinger   111

are brought around at last to accepting roles as participants
in the human community.

The similarities between the two novels suggest that
the element in the American population sensitive enough to
be moved by probing dramatizations of our national condition
as a reflection of the human condition both immediately before and after World War II shared the vision of achieving
universal brotherhood that underlies in the United Nations
charter. Whereas the readers of the depressed 1930's, however, were cheered by this vision, the readers of the afflu-
ent 1950's were depressed by it. I suspect that such fluctua-
tions must continue if we are to have any ideals at all. Human brotherhood must remain something toward which individuals strive, not something imposed upon us by a com-
mittee, if the reading of writers like Salinger and Steinbeck
is to continue to have any meaning for us. Otherwise we
are likely to sink into the supine inertia of Steinbeck's Ethan
Allen Hawley in The Winter of Our Discontent or succumb
to the suicidal impulses of Salinger's Seymour Glass, "daz-
zled to death by his own scruples, the blinding shapes and
colors of his own sacred human conscience. "

During his movement from alienation-to-acceptance,
Steinbeck had produced his own version of Seymour Glass in
Tortilla Flat (1935). Steinbeck's Danny expiates his having
become the slave of property in the way that Seymour conceives he might become the slave of respectability by battling
to death against a "worthy" enemy. Those who Danny has
left behind at a party hear his "last shrill cry of defiance. "
Then "answering challenge so fearful and so chill that their
spines wilted like nasturtium stems under frost. " Then silence. "Even now, " Steinbeck writes, "when people speak
of Danny's opponent, they lower their voices and look fur-
tively about. " Arthur F. Kinney supposes that "Danny gets
so drunk that he topples in stupor over a cliff to his death, "[4]
but this literal-minded interpretation trivializes a deceptively
droll attempt to create a legend that might serve as a modern Morte d'Arthur, in case there were any demand for one.

Danny's "worthy opponent" is not drink, but the mid-
dle-class respectability associated with property that Steinbeck attacked with such vigor in all his novels through Cannery Row (1945), but which he later defended with such vigor
in The Winter of Our Discontent, once he became a New York
landholder himself.

There is a difference, however, in Steinbeck and Salinger's attachment to the figure who chooses death over reconciliation with a materialistic world. Salinger remained
fascinated with the self-conscious martyr as long as he chose
to remain in communication with the world. His first and
last really successful stories, "A Perfect Day for Banana-
fish" and "Seymour: An Introduction" are concerned with
this figure. Steinbeck, however, was able to put Danny behind him. In In Dubious Battle (1936) and Of Mice and Men
(1937), innocent, generous persons are sacrificed, but Steinbeck attributes their destruction to the perversities of a decadent world that because of financial or sexual obsessions
cannot allow innocence to flourish. Steinbeck's works before
The Grapes of Wrath are all modern-dress version of the
Christian story of martyrdom and redemption, and the tor-
mentors are direct descendants of the Biblical pharisees.

In The Grapes of Wrath, the sacrificial figure is rather blatantly identified as a new Christ by his initials, his
speeches, and the parallels that a throng of critics have already pointed out. [5] By the time, however, that Steinbeck
produced his last novel, he was willing to attempt the task
that Salinger would have found impossible of converting Seymour Glass into Holden Caulfield by having Ethan Allen Hawley, who seems to have been headed for a Seymour-Glass-
like self-destruction, make a last-minute decision to humiliate
himself before the world in order to protect his young daughter. Fatherhood is rarely compatible with martyrdom.

One might say that Steinbeck's increasing success in
accommodating himself to the world as he achieved success
and Salinger's increasing withdrawal from the world in the
face of similar success are just illustrative of the different
behavior patterns of unrelated men; but in view of the facts
that writers of distinction are rare at any time and that
these two men did produce works with unique appeals to the
American public, it is impossible to suppose that we are
not dealing with similar specimens of a rare breed.

I think that the behavior of Steinbeck and Salinger reflects a dramatic, perhaps catastrophic change in American
sentiment during the period that included World War II.
Steinbeck started out in The Pastures of Heaven (1932) and
To A God Unknown (1933) as a distinctly disaffiliated writer,
expressing the horror of a mercenary society that the Beats
and Hippies would later express. But as society welcomed
his works, he (like S. I. Hayakawa in another field) warmed

up to society and ended his duties as a word-magician by
playing Wizard of Id to little King Lyndon Johnson and his
"Americanize the Universe" policies.

Salinger, on the other hand, as is evident from his
little-known early contributions to Story magazine and his political conservatism began as a writer with a distaste for the
"Establishment" who still thought that it must be served and
ended up as an advocate of total disassociation, even extend-
ing to the suicide of sensitive individuals who could not rec-
oncile themselves to a squalid world.

These changes in position reflect, I feel, broad
changes in the attitude of sensitive, thoughtful Americans
(despite the proliferation of Suburbia there remain a few)
over the middle third of the twentieth century.   In the 1930's
most Americans were isolationists who were brought around
at last to a belief that one does have a duty to his fellow
man to make sacrifices in the name of humanity.   Just as
the turgid-minded public was coming around to this position
that thoughtful persons had embraced earlier, the thoughtful
spectators of the aftermath of World War II were adopting
the position that to surrender one's self to society was literally to destroy one's self as an individual--physically and
spiritually.   The only escapes were--for the irrepressible
spirits like Seymour Glass to beat society to the punch and
commit suicide, for less volatile personalities like Seymour's
brother Buddy to isolate one's self completely and spend one's
life in monastic devotion to the departed Messiah.   (Few could
accept Steinbeck's attitude that one must transform the President of the United States into this Messiah and isolate one's
self from everyone but him.)

This attitude of Steinbeck's provides an answer to the
final question that must confront anyone comparing him with
Salinger: why did he keep pounding out increasingly poorer
copy until the very end of his life whereas Salinger seems
to have been driven early into permanent silence?

Steinbeck, I feel, as a result of the acclaim accorded
The Grapes of Wrath, came to conceive of himself as one of
what Shelley calls "the unacknowledged legislators, " and then
--as his friendship with Lyndon Johnson developed--one of
the semi-acknowledged ones.   Steinbeck, in short, in spite
of his aloofness to his admirers, was "available" if the call
came from high enough.   Salinger, on the other hand, having
been scared out of his wits by the adulation accorded him

after the publication of The Catcher in the Rye, felt it necessary to wall himself altogether off from the world, trusting
at first the high-schoolers, but excluding even them when he
felt betrayed. Both courses, I feel, augur ill for our society; perhaps we cannot hope for a person who can speak to
the world both through his imaginative creations and in his
own person.

There is finally a difference between the scope of the
men's writing. This discussion has contrasted what is only
a single--though important--thread in Steinbeck's work with
the central concern of the stories on which Salinger's reputation rests. Steinbeck is an extensive writer, whereas Salinger is an intensive one. Even this difference suggests a
reason for their changing patterns of behavior. Steinbeck
saw an increasing need for messiahs invoked by word-magic,
and he attempted to speed up the manufacture of linguistic
icons with the not unusual result that his final products were
little more than parodies of his earlier ones. Unmoved by
the demand of the market, on the other hand, and depressed
at the thought that if society should discover a new messiah
it would only destroy him, Salinger shut up shop.

I resent scoffing statements that Steinbeck and Salinger
are not outstanding writers, despite obvious limitations of
their work. Neither is an artist like Faulkner who is able
to transcend the limitations of time and space and to find universal drama in his environment, but how many such writers
are there? Are we not to value also those whose stumbling
efforts may stimulate our own vision?

Despite their differences, Steinbeck and Salinger have
not just distracted us with whimsical trivialities; they have
let us see what was happening to sensitive, troubled people
at the times each was at the height of his power. Salinger,
in fact, replaces Steinbeck's concept that god is all men
with the idea that each man must be god. "Maybe all men
got one big soul ever'body's a part of, " preacher Casy says,
echoing Emerson. "I am giving Sister Irma her freedom to
follow her own destiny. Everybody is a nun, " Salinger's De-
Daumier Smith notes in his diary.

Notes

1. See Warren French A Companion to "The Grapes of
   Wrath" (New York, 1963, pp. 105-111) for a summa-

tion of these reviews, especially Clifton Fadiman's in
the New Yorker.   Fadiman was at that time fancied
the principal arbiter of refined reading tastes.

2.   Aldridge presented the often repeated argument that Hold-
     en Caulfield "remains at the end what he was at the
     beginning--cynical, defiant, and blind. " Aldridge's re-
     marks, along with a variety of other interpretations
     of Holden's behavior, are collected in Harold P. Si-
     monson and Philip E. Hager (eds.), Salinger's "Catch-
     er in the Rye": Clamor vs. Criticism (Boston, 1963).

3.   Thornton Wilder in The Eighth Day (New York, 1967),
     pp. 326-77, discusses the profoundly disturbing effects
     of the break-up of the old patriarchal order on our
     society.   The novel, in fact, is shaped around a spe-
     cific act that symbolizes this break-up and the inabili-
     ty of "traditional-minded" people even to perceive the
     truth about this incident.

4.   "The Arthurian Cycle in Tortilla Flat, " Modern Fiction
     Studies, 11 (Spring 1965), 11-20.

5.   Agnes McNeill Donohue's A Casebook on "The Grapes of
     Wrath" (New York, 1968), pp. 90-117, reprints the
     major articles discussing the use of Biblical symbol-
     ism in the novel.   The earliest of them, Martin
     Staples Shockley's "Christian Symbolism in The Grapes
     of Wrath, " College English, 17 (1956), 87-90, remains
     the most comprehensive.

9. STEINBECK AND ADLAI STEVENSON

John Steinbeck and Adlai Stevenson: The Shattered Image of America
by Sanford E. Marovitz

I

Deeply embedded in the American consciousness glimmers a spark of wanderlust. Perhaps it was set aglowing by America's immigrant history, for not far back in the ancestry of most Americans, someone broke free from his cultural ties and crossed an ocean into the New World. Whatever the cause, let the spark be fanned by the breeze of circumstance, and it becomes an infernal flame that devours newspaper travel sections and is controlled only by hastening for the far side of the globe.

In the autumn of 1960 the gleam led John Steinbeck over ten thousand miles and through thirty-four states. [1] His journey should have been a happy one, but his account of it in Travels with Charley in Search of America is surely one of the most disheartening best-sellers to appear in this country since the publication of The Grapes of Wrath in 1939. Steinbeck set out on his transamerican journey as a knight-errant hoping to celebrate his country, and he returned a nerve-wracked, disenchanted Ishmael lost in a nation full of isolates and fear-inspired anxieties. It is easy enough to recognize why James Woodress has dismissed Steinbeck's narrative as "a witty, entertaining, but shallow travelogue"-- "a pot-boiling disappointment"[2]--because, as he explains, the book contains too much about the author and not enough about his subject. I refer here to Travels with Charley not to offer praise where little praise is due, but to suggest, rather, that in revealing more than expected about the author himself, the book possibly exposes a weakness that may paradoxically be its strength.

Ensconced behind the wheel of his factory-new, custom-ordered camper--appropriately yclept "Rocinante"--

Steinbeck set off in September, 1960. With his French poo-
dle, Charley, and spare tanks filled with extra water, butane,
and alcohol (for consumption, not combustion), 3 he intended
to explore the brave new world which he would chauvinistical-
ly display four years later in America and Americans (1966),
a coffee-table caravan of photographs and uninspired text.
His journey was not a pleasant one, for he soon observed--
to his increasing dismay--that his beautiful land was inhabited
by relatively few beautiful people; and it is clear that if Travels with Charley originated as a quest for confirmation of
American nobility, it ended with the realization that the
American dream could seldom be seen but with one's eyes
tightly closed against prevailing nightmarish realities--racism,
hypocrisy, and the sickening sterility of a plastic-coated country.

        The shattering effect of Steinbeck's circumambulatory
journey through America seems to have been the inevitable
result of his vision of man as animal finally converging with
his vision of man as compassionate idealist and Christian.
The consequent meeting eventuated in fission, not fusion; and
that the lack of synthesis had an enduring detrimental effect
on the author--Nobel Prize winner or not--is only too evident in the work of his last fifteen to eighteen years. 4 If
Steinbeck made us aware of American social ailments in In
Dubious Battle and The Grapes of Wrath, both written during
the 1930's, so did he also have faith then that the American
people would strive to correct the wrongs he had exposed.
In a sense, American activity during the Second World War
confirmed his faith and justified his pride in his country; in
The Grapes of Wrath he had written:

        For man, unlike any other thing, organic or inor-
        ganic, in the universe, grows beyond his work....
        Having stepped forward, he may slip back, but
        only half a step, never the full step back.... This
        you may know when the bombs plummet out of the
        black planes on the market place, when prisoners
        are stuck like pigs, when the crushed bodies drain
        filthily in the dust.... If the step were not being
        taken, if the stumbling-forward ache were not
        alive, the bombs would not fall, the throats would
        not be cut. Fear the time when the bombs stop
        falling while the bombers live--for every bomb is
        proof that the spirit has not died. And ... fear
        the time when Manself will not suffer and die for
        a concept, for this one quality is the foundation of

Manself, and this one quality is man, distinctive
in the universe. 5

Two years after the appearance of this declaration of faith
in man, the United States entered World War II and put it to
the test.

The sudden death of F. D. R. in April, 1945, only a
few months after the beginning of his fourth term in office,
left Harry Truman in the White House; and the lackadaisical
1948 campaign of Governor Thomas E. Dewey of New York,
based on his foolish and unwarranted optimism, assured the
Democrats of the Presidency for at least another four years.
During the Republican Convention of 1952, memories of the
war were revivified, and the American people were reminded that not all old soldiers, as it were, "fade away"; despite
his lack of political experience, General Dwight Eisenhower
was selected on the first ballot to run as candidate for President on the Republican ticket. His public image as a victori-
ous military commander--indeed, a war hero--was an attribute not to be dismissed in favor of a more accomplished
politician's program; and Eisenhower charged into the campaign with a winning smile, the catch phrase "It's time for
a change," and a platform split by party dissension.

Among the many millions of voters attracted to the
old soldier's image was John Steinbeck, a former war correspondent of the European and African campaigns, who recalled that "President Harding stirred me toward the Democratic party and President Hoover cemented me there."6
Steinbeck's attraction to Eisenhower, however, like that of
most American voters, is not difficult to comprehend when
one realizes that few people had heard of his opponent before the Democratic Convention in July. Adlai E. Stevenson
was highly regarded in Illinois, where, as Governor, he had
done much to clean up syndicated gambling and political
graft; but outside his own state he was simply unknown. "A
year and a half ago, I had never heard of Mr. Stevenson,"
Steinbeck wrote late in 1952. "A year ago I knew his name
and only remembered it because of the unusual first name.
Until the convention I had never heard nor read a Stevenson-
ian word. And now we hurry through dinner to hear him on
radio or to see him on television."7 Steinbeck's shift from
Eisenhower--whom he had been "solidly behind"--was quick
and dramatic. He indicated the reason for his rapid change
in the foreword to a collection of Stevenson's campaign
speeches published during the autumn of 1952. "I have

switched entirely because of the speeches, " he explained,
and continued:

> A man cannot think muddled and write clear. Day
> by day it has seemed to me that Eisenhower's
> speeches have become more formless and mixed
> up and uncertain. ... Eisenhower seems to have
> lost the ability to take any kind of stand on any
> subject. ... Stevenson, on the other hand, has
> touched no political, economic, or moral subject
> on which he has not taken a clear and open stand
> even to the point of bearding selfish groups to
> their faces.
>
> ... With equal pressures we have seen in a pitiful
> few months the Eisenhower mind crumble into un-
> certainty, retire into generalities, fumble with
> friendships and juggle alliances. At the same
> time Stevenson has moved serenely on, clarifying
> his position, holding to his line and never being
> drawn nor driven from his nongeneralized ideals.
>
> ... As a writer I love the clear, clean writing of
> Stevenson. As a man I like his intelligent, hu-
> morous, logical, civilized mind. [8]

For Steinbeck, Adlai Stevenson was the ideal political
leader, a man with the integrity and ability to guide the
American people in a way that might help them restrain
their perpetual restlessness from dissipating their energy
and canceling out one action by another in a continuum of
profitless paradoxes. "We are a restless, a dissatisfied, a
searching people, " Steinbeck wrote in America and Americans:

> We bridle and buck under failure, and we go mad
> with dissatisfaction in the face of success. ... We
> work too hard, and many die under the strain; and
> then to make up for that we play with a violence
> as suicidal.
>
> The result is that we seem to be in a state of tur-
> moil all the time, both physically and mentally. ...
>
> The paradoxes are everywhere: We shout that we
> are a nation of laws, not men--and then proceed
> to break every law we can if we can get away with
> it. We proudly insist that we have our political

positions on the issues--and we will vote against a
man because of his religion, his name, or the shape
of his nose. 9

Steinbeck believed that this restless urge for action was deeply infused in the American character; in "The Leader of the
People, " Jody's grandfather still dreams nostalgically of his
Western passage, and long after it was done he gazed at
length out over the Pacific as though he were ready to set
sail and continue pushing forward.

Stevenson himself shared this spirit.   Like Steinbeck,
he thrived well in the outdoors; indeed, Steinbeck's daemon
seems to have been guiding Stevenson's pen as he wrote to
a friend during his campaign for Governor of Illinois in 1948:

I've seen Illinois in a capsule--the beauty of the
south, the fruit belt, the coal fields, the oil fields,
the great industrial area around East St. Louis--
and everywhere the rich, black, fecund earth
stretching away and away.   It gives you a great
feeling of pride and power.   Shut your eyes for a
moment and let the fetid, hot places, the scorched
islands, the arid, the cold, the small--all the
places of the world where men struggle to live and
love and breed--dance through your head.   Then
open your eyes and look at Illinois, and murmur
'thrice blessed land. '10

"I own farm land in Illinois, " Stevenson reminded his
listeners at the National Plowing Contest in Kasson, Minnesota (June 9, 1952), "and I come from a family that has
lived in the heart of the farm belt for over a hundred years. "11
A favorite photograph of himself was snapped while he sat at
the wheel of a tractor, which he could manipulate well; to
be sure, he was adept at all the tasks of a farmer and
could handle the tools accordingly.   Again like Steinbeck, he
enjoyed camping and hunting; Mrs. Edison Dick, an old
family friend, recalled that

Adlai loved to ride and on snowy Sundays he would
hitch up one of the horses and take his family
sleighriding.... He showed little boys how to
trap and fish along the river bank.   They hunted
arrowheads in the meadow, and he enlivened canoe
trips with tall tales about the Indians. 12

Mrs. Dick's description suggests glimpses of a reincarnated
Thoreau, whose affection for youngsters was often exhibited
in a similar manner.   Another delightful photograph displays
Stevenson with his three sons, each bearing a shotgun and a
hunter's smile of satisfaction over the ring-necked pheasants
they had brought down shortly before. [13]

        Obviously, however, it was not his prowess with a
canoe paddle or a shotgun that led Steinbeck to regard the
Democratic candidate as a political savior of America.   Perhaps leaning a little too heavily on exaggeration for effect,
Steinbeck charged that until Stevenson emerged to the Presi-
dential candidacy, "politics--the word, the practice--had become disreputable to the point where politics and crime
were confused in many minds.   The career of a politician
was for the greedy, the unscrupulous," he continued, in
language more than a little like that of Lincoln Steffens,
whose muckraking articles for <u>McClure's</u> at the beginning of
the century shocked citizens into disbelief over the enormity
of big-city political graft.   "Men of ideals and conscience
avoided politics as an arena where wolves tore at the body
of the nation and snapped and snarled at each other," Steinbeck wrote to Stevenson, not long after Adlai's defeat in
1952.   "Then, in a few short months, you ... changed that
picture.   You made it seem possible for politics to be as it
once had been, an honorable, virtuous and creative business."[14]

        In the light of his resounding defeats by Eisenhower,
it seems doubtful that Stevenson could have done anything
whatever during the campaigns that would have altered the
results significantly enough to put him in the White House;
nevertheless, it is possible that his outspoken honesty in
1952 lost him more votes than it gained.   "Let's talk sense
to the American people," he reiterated in one speech after
another; and drawing upon a Kantian ethic, he stated un-
equivocably to his audience in Richmond: "We must do right
for right's sake alone."[15]   In Baltimore he told his listeners
that if he is elected there is going to be "no pork-barreling
while our economy is in its present condition.   If your principal interest in life is getting a new federally financed boon-
doggle for your state you had better vote for somebody
else."[16]   And to the automobile workers in Detroit:

        Labor unions must conform to standards of fair
        conduct and equal protection in the exercise of
        stewardship.   A few unions ... abuse [their] trust

> by excluding from membership some who want to
> work, denying them a vote, denying their seniority
> rights because of the color of their skin or be-
> cause of restrictive notions about employment se-
> curity. That's not right.

And a few moments later: "We cannot ... tolerate shut-
downs which threaten our national safety, even that of the
whole free world. The right to bargain collectively does
not include a right to stop the national economy. "[17]

What becomes increasingly apparent to a reader of
Stevenson's campaign speeches as he moves page by page
with the speaker across the nation, is that Stevenson--mor-
ally correct, of course, but politically suicidal--spoke to
the American people as if they constituted a thoroughly enlightened electorate having more concern with far-reaching
legitimate issues than with public images and self-interest.
As an honest man, however, Stevenson had no choice. He
wrote:

> To trade integrity for a quick promotion or to
> sacrifice self-respect and conviction for the boss'
> favor is a price I would not pay. Better to be
> fired for the right cause than to sell your talents
> for the wrong one. You won't have an opportunity
> to try out your ideas and ideals, unless you resist
> the temptation to sell them out. Conscience is a
> fragile thing. [18]

Using the vigorous aphoristic style of Emerson, Stevenson
brought the virtues of nineteenth-century Transcendentalism
into twentieth-century politics. He was the embodiment of
Jefferson's "natural aristocrat, " blessed as he was with virtue and talents; Lowell would have considered him a true
"gentleman, " and Whitman would have declared him a poet--
perhaps the poet, the seer, for whom America was waiting.

II

If Stevenson was disillusioned with the American people after the elections, he seldom revealed it in public.
Like Jefferson, he recognized the essential value of an enlightened electorate in a free democracy, and even after his
defeat in 1952 he continued to promote his view that a

genuinely free and an honestly informed people will

> ultimately triumph over intolerance, injustice and
> evil from without or within. But a lazy people, an
> apathetic people, an uninformed people or a people
> too proud for politics, is not free. And [he added],
> it may quickly be a mob. [19]

In an address delivered at Harvard the previous year, his
American idealism fairly glowed:

> Poverty, oppression and ignorance have always
> been our concern, and those who see virtue only
> in self-interest and self-preservation mistake, I
> think, our character and misread our history. . . .
> A propitious political accident . . . has made our
> inborn compassion co-ordinate with the national
> interest. [20]

Stevenson refused to be satisfied with the apparent
American tendency--indeed, world tendency--to strive might-
ily for, and to a large extent achieve, mastery over natural
forces while moral concerns remained ignored and buried beneath increasing piles of atomic waste. "After all," he
wrote in 1955, "the great issues of the day are not technical,
they are moral."[21] Steinbeck agreed, emphasizing the pernicious fear generated by the atomic revolution: "And just as
surely as we are poisoning the air with our test bombs," he
observed in his Introduction to Once There Was a War (1958),
"so are we poisoned in our souls by fear, faceless, stupid
sarcomic terror."[22] Stevenson, in contrast, found the new
atomic technology awesome but not necessarily fearful, for
atomic power is of nature, and nature is neutral. "In any
case," he said, "let us not cower with fear before this new
instrument of power. . . . There is no evil in the atom: only
in men's souls. . . . The way to deal with evil men has never varied; stand up for the right, and if needs must be, fight
for the right."[23] Reasserting the high value of American
democracy in a world at once menaced and blessed with
man's new control over atomic power, Stevenson proclaimed
that the United States must never disregard "the moral sentiments of human liberty and human welfare embodied in the
Declaration of Independence and the Bill of Rights."[24] Over
and over, Stevenson extolled the intrinsic virtues of a "thriv-
ing, full-bodied democracy,"[25] which he defined as "honest
disagreement, . . . liberty coupled with responsibility,"[26] a
means of self-government in which "all the people reason together, reason aloud, reason their way to clarity of judgment
and unity of purpose."[27]

Stevenson's constant appeal to the moral intelligence of the common citizen made a strong impact on Steinbeck, who regarded himself as one of the "so-called 'people'" all his life.28 "We always underrate the intelligence of the 'people,'" he observed in 1952;29 and later, in Travels with Charley, he confessed: "I admire all nations and hate all governments."30 But if one can judge from the rest of his traveler's tale, Steinbeck's affection for the people was projected with more lip-service than soul. It was difficult for him to maintain faith in a nation of withdrawn materialists, each hunting his own Great Carbuncle composed of plastic and smelling of cash. In a published letter to Stevenson, written upon his return from England and less than a year before he commenced his peregrination in "Rocinante," Steinbeck itemized his two "first impressions" of America after an extended stay abroad:

> First, a creeping, all pervading, nerve-gas of immorality which starts in the nursery and does not stop before it reaches the highest offices, both corporate and governmental. Two, a nervous restlessness, a hunger, a thirst, a yearning for something unknown--perhaps morality. Then there's the violence, cruelty and a hypocrisy symptomatic of a people which has too much, and last, the surly, ill temper which only shows up in humans when they are frightened.31

Throughout the letter he excoriated the pervasive immorality and materialistic values that he had observed in his native land, and he concluded that

> Someone has to reinspect our system.... We can't expect to raise our children to be good and honorable men when the city, the state, the government, the corporations all offer higher rewards for chicanery and deceit than for probity and truth. On all levels it is rigged, Adlai. Maybe nothing can be done about it, but I am stupid enough and naively hopeful enough to want to try.32

The weak ray of hope expressed in his concluding line probably points directly to the underlying purpose of his nomadic journey. Stung by Stevenson's two defeats and despondent over the malignancies he had perceived in American society-- "On all levels it is rigged," he had written--Steinbeck needed to go back among the people and discover whether the fault lay with the nation or the government.

The issue of a "rigged" morality was nothing new to
Stevenson. If he was "resolutely idealistic on issues," as
Stephen A. Mitchell has suggested, so was he also "realistic
about politics and politicians."[33] In America and Americans,
Steinbeck recalled an incident that had occurred between
Stevenson and Sam Rayburn: Stevenson had insisted upon an
open convention to elect the Vice-Presidential candidate, and
Rayburn countered that he had to be appointed. When Rayburn finally relented after hours of debate, he said sadly but
kindly to Adlai: "Look, son--look Governor--I'm an old
man, and I've been through this for many years, and I tell
you I don't mind an open convention--as long as it's rigged!"[34]
Who can distinguish with certainty the truth from the humor
in Rayburn's statement? Could Stevenson? Having spent no
little time in state politics before being drafted as the Presi-
dential candidate in 1952, Stevenson, like most Americans,
he said, had become

> accustomed to political bad manners and billings-
> gate. After a century and a half we have developed
> some immunity to vilification, abuse and misrep-
> resentation in our domestic public dialogue. If not
> an ornament to the American tradition it is at
> least a part of it, and we have learned somehow
> to give it a rough evaluation and get along surpris-
> ingly well in spite of deceit, demagoguery and ver-
> bal violence.[35]

Stevenson's eclectic reading and dry wit usually en-
abled him to treat demagoguery with irony and thereby coun-
terattack with barbed sarcasm. He "was the undefeated
champion of the deflating retort, the complete squelch and
the droll epigram,"[36] Newton N. Minow has recalled; and
Steinbeck, too, like many of Stevenson's associates and ac-
quaintances, appreciated his brand of controlled humor. After
pointing out that political jests are usually contrived, irrelevant, and flat enough to avoid infury by implication, Steinbeck noted that Stevenson had changed the technique by "draw
[ing] his humor from his subject. His jokes, far from ob-
scuring his message, enlighten it."[37] If Stevenson was not
aware of Mark Twain's dictum (expressed in The Mysterious
Stranger) that the "one really effective weapon" of mankind
is laughter, he learned the lesson elsewhere and employed
it throughout his political and diplomatic career.

Likewise, Steinbeck's mind often turned to comedy.
John Kenneth Galbraith had known him but a short time before recognizing that he was "not only droll but very, very
funny. "38 Steinbeck once requested, for example, that Galbraith arrange to have him appointed as the American Am-
bassador to Oz.   "Now Oz has another secret weapon we
could well use on all levels of government and diplomacy, "
Steinbeck wrote in a letter to Galbraith.   "The Wizard of Oz
is a fraud who admits he is a fraud. Can you think what
this would do if it got into chancelleries and general staffs[?]
There would be a major break-through. "39 Deception and
greed were constant topics of conversation and letters between Steinbeck and Galbraith, and often the subjects were
treated with caustic irony.

But by 1960, the comedy had worn thin. The knight-
errant who returned from his cross-country trek in "Rocinante" was, indeed, "the Knight of the Woeful Countenance"--
a disenchanted Don Quixote with no prospects of finding his
lost Dulcinea.   Like a self-styled Dante, Steinbeck had descended through the Circles of the Inferno and emerged to
find that Paradise was not in the offing and Beatrice did not
exist.   Although Stevenson, in contrast, never forgot or for-
gave the shattering dishonor of his experience following the
Bay of Pigs fiasco in 1961, the episode did not lead to a
continued loss of faith. Having been deceived, he confessed
to an associate: "My credibility has been compromised, and
therefore my usefulness. Yet how can I resign at this moment, " he asked, "and make things still worse for the President?"40 He did not resign, of course; his "inner core of
indestructible strength"41 had continued to support him, and
his fatal collapse on a London street in 1965 marked the de-
mise of an ideal American and "a universal man. "42 Steinbeck's death in 1968, however, came when his glory, even
as a winner of the Nobel Prize, was waning fast. His best
work was decades behind him, and he seems to have suc-
cumbed to the materialism he had often condemned. Steinbeck's star rose, gleamed brilliantly, and fell, leaving in
its wake a broken dusty trail; Stevenson's star, on the contrary, did not climb as high, did not shine as brightly, but
remained clear and steadfast to the end. Together their
beams projected America's golden image to the world.

Notes

1.   John Steinbeck, Travels with Charley in Search of

America (New York: Viking, 1962), p. 7; hereafter
cited as Travels with Charley.

2. "John Steinbeck: Hostage to Fortune," in A Casebook on
   "The Grapes of Wrath," ed. Agnes McNeill Donohue
   (New York: Thomas Y. Crowell, 1968), p. 289.

3. John Kenneth Galbraith has remarked that Steinbeck was
   a "controlled drinker," who liked to think of his cock-
   tail hour as "Milking Time"; see "John Steinbeck:
   Footnote for a Memoir," The Atlantic, 224 (November 1969), 66; hereafter cited as "Memoir." Mr.
   Galbraith's amusing personal account of Steinbeck as
   an acquaintance is much fairer than the unrelieved
   character assassination recently published in Esquire
   by George Frazier, in which the vainglorious reflection of the author himself displays a far more trifling
   and inane image than the distorted portrait of his
   subject; see (or better still, do not bother to see)
   "John Steinbeck! John Steinbeck! How Still We See
   Thee Lie and Lie, and Lie," Esquire, 72 (November 1969), 150, 269, 271, 274-5.

4. See Peter Lisca's very perceptive analysis: "Steinbeck's
   Image of Man and His Decline as a Writer," Modern
   Fiction Studies, 11 (Spring 1965), 3-10.

5. The Grapes of Wrath (New York: Viking Compass
   Edition, 1958), pp. 204-5.

6. Travels with Charley, p. 177.

7. Foreword to Speeches of Adlai Stevenson (New York:
   Random House, 1952), p. 5; hereafter cited as
   Speeches. This paperback collection of Stevenson's
   1952 campaign speeches is not an easy book to find,
   and I should here like to express my appreciation to
   my brother, James, for his help, and to my mother,
   Mrs. Harold Marovitz, who traipsed through many a
   Chicago book store for me before she finally discovered a copy.

8. Ibid., pp. 7-8.

9. America and Americans (New York: Viking, 1966), pp.
   29-30.

10. Jane Warner Dick, "Forty Years of Friendship, " in As We Knew Adlai: The Stevenson Story by Twenty-Two Friends (New York: Harper & Row, 1966), p. 276; hereafter cited as As We Knew Adlai.

11. Speeches, p. 64.

12. As We Knew Adlai, p. 270.

13. Both photographs have been reproduced in As We Knew Adlai, pp. 271, 273.

14. "The 'Stevenson Spirit, '" in The Faces of Five Decades, Selected from Fifty Years of the New Republic: 1914-1964, ed. Robert B. Luce (New York: Simon & Schuster, 1964), p. 334. (Originally published January 5, 1953.) It may be suggested that Steinbeck's choice here of the word "business" is rather unfortunate and inappropriate, but one can be sure that he employed it in a figurative rather than a literal sense and implied nothing sarcastic or derogatory by it.

15. Speeches, p. 90.

16. Ibid. , p. 124.

17. Ibid. , pp. 54-5.

18. "If I Were Twenty-one, " in Fabulous Yesterday: Coronet's 25th Anniversary Album, ed. Lewis W. Gellenson (New York: Harper & Row, 1961), p. 166; hereafter cited as "If I Were Twenty-one. " (Originally published December, 1955.)

19. Ibid. , p. 165.

20. "Perpetual Peril, " in Call to Greatness (New York: Atheneum, 1966), p. 75; hereafter cited as Call to Greatness. (Addresses originally delivered March 17-19, 1954, at Harvard University.)

21. "If I Were Twenty-one, " p. 165.

22. Once There Was a War (New York: Viking, 1958), p. xx.

23. Speeches, p. 97.

24. Call to Greatness, p. 108.

25. "If I Were Twenty-one, " p. 165.

26. Stevenson's definition of democracy is not quoted but
    paraphrased by Barry Bingham, "With Adlai in Asia, "
    in As We Knew Adlai, p. 194.

27. "If I Were Twenty-one, " p. 165.

28. Foreword to Speeches, p. 6.

29. Ibid. , p. 5.

30. Travels with Charley, p. 76.

31. Adlai E. Stevenson and John Steinbeck, "Our 'Rigged'
    Morality, " in Fabulous Yesterday, p. 198. (Origi-
    nally published March, 1960.)

32. Ibid.

33. "Adlai's Amateurs, " in As We Knew Adlai, p. 66.

34. America and Americans, p. 45.

35. Call to Greatness, p. 33.

36. "Marching to the Beat of Mankind, " in As We Knew
    Adlai, p. 183.

37. Foreword to Speeches, p. 6.

38. "Memoir, " p. 65.

39. Ibid. , p. 67.

40. Jane Warner Dick, in As We Knew Adlai, p. 286.

41. Barbara Ward, "'Affection and Always Respect, '" in
    As We Knew Adlai, p. 224.

42. David Dean Rusk (Secretary of State), quoted by Francis
    T. P. Plimpton, "They Sent You Our Best, " in As
    We Knew Adlai, p. 267.

10. STEINBECK AND ROBERT PENN WARREN

John Steinbeck's In Dubious Battle and
Robert Penn Warren's Night Rider: A Comparative Study
by George Henry Spies III

In 1936 John Steinbeck published his fifth novel, In
Dubious Battle. This powerful and controversial book is a
timely study of violence, labor strife, and one man's personal involvement in conflicting sociological and psychological forces. Three years later, Robert Penn Warren's first
novel Night Rider was published. In it Warren utilized many
of the themes and concepts that are dominant in Steinbeck's
novel. Both authors, in fact, deal with similar ideas in
that they investigate themes intimately connected with modern society: business monopolies, terrorist groups, the
crowd as a social force, alienation from society, and the
loss of moral values.

In a sense both Steinbeck and Warren can be considered "regionalists." Their best novels and short stories are
concerned with the psychological and sociological problems
indigenous to their particular native regions, California for
Steinbeck and Kentucky for Warren. 1 Because of their intimate knowledge of the people from their respective birth-
places, both writers are able to dramatize vividly and sympathetically the plights of the migrant workers and the tobacco planters. Even though the events in the novels are sepa-
rated in distance by 2500 miles and in time by thirty years,
Steinbeck writing about his own adult generation of the 1930's
and Warren concerned with the previous one of the early
1900's, the problems of the "fruit tramps" are strikingly
similar to the plight of the tobacco farmers. Both groups
represent the oppressed "working class" who have been
abused by ruthless monopolies throughout history; in Steinbeck's In Dubious Battle, the evil power is the Fruit Growers' Association while in Warren's Night Rider it is the all-
powerful Tobacco Trust. In both the imaginary Torgas Valley in central California and the tobacco-growing region in

southern Kentucky a kind of feudal state is created in which
these monopolies force the workers to take the minimum pay
for their products and services.

In Steinbeck's In Dubious Battle, the author asserts
that wealthy fruit growers own most of central California.
They are therefore absolute monarchs of their land and
"rule" as they see fit. Mac, the tough Party agitator, expresses the situation accurately when he says: "This valley's
organized like Italy."[2] In relating the situation to Jim, his
novice co-worker, Mac complains:

> They got this valley organized. God how they've
> got it organized. It's not so hard to do when a
> few men control everything, land, courts, banks.
> They can cut off loans, and they can railroad a
> man to jail, and they can always bribe plenty [167-
> 168].

The wealthy fruit growers are efficiently organized and have
their subterfuge well planned. They wait until migrant fruit
pickers go to the expense and trouble of moving themselves
and their families to the valley. When the workers are set-
tled the announcement is made that the wages promised earlier are to be lowered. Thus, the "fruit tramps" are caught.
Unless they can afford to leave the valley immediately, they
are forced to stay and pick the fruit at an unreasonably low
wage rate. Naturally the Fruit Growers' Association usually
gets its way and the workers can do no more than grumble
about the deceitful and dehumanizing transaction.

The same basic situation exists in Kentucky for the
poor tobacco farmers in Night Rider. The injustice here
stems from the corrupt trusts setting the tobacco price; this
automatically rules out a competitive process of buying.
The buyers for the Tobacco Trust yearly force low prices
on the helpless farmers. The Trust considers neither the
economic needs of the planters nor the true commercial
worth of the tobacco; it is concerned only with buying the
product at the lowest possible price. Bill Christian laments
the plight of his fellow planters by heatedly crying, "It's
been ten years since tobacco got a fair price, and the land
in this section's all mortgaged, and half the folks nigh starving."[3] Thus, Warren's tobacco farmers are ruthlessly exploited in almost the same manner as Steinbeck's fruit pickers. Both monopolies are as cold-blooded and malicious as
the law allows.

After realizing the deplorable circumstances under
which both groups of people exist, one can comprehend the
hostility and frustration that produce violence. Incensed by
the low prices offered for their crops, the planters in Night
Rider found a protective association to negotiate with the Tobacco Trust. When negotiation proves too slow and ineffec-
tive a process, they organize the Free Farmers' Brotherhood
of Protection and Control, a secret fraternal order better
known in the novel as the "night riders. " This terrorist
group, ironically referred to as Le bras pour de droit ("The
arm for the right") (143), destroys the plant beds of farmers
who refuse to join the tobacco strike planned by the Association. Later in their campaign to get their demands, the
"night riders" even carry out military operations bent on de-
railing trains, dynamiting bridges, and burning warehouses.

Like the Kentucky planters, the California fruit pickers yearn for justice through effective leadership.   They get
it from what Steinbeck calls the "Party. "[4] Jim and Mac
gather the workers together, incite them to anger, and finally organize a strike against the Fruit Growers' Association.
Both strikes, however, are doomed to failure because the
monopolies have the law on their side and can inflict terrible
reprisals on the workers if necessary. For instance, in
both novels the National Guard is called out to squelch the
violent protesters.   Not only do they accomplish this, but
they also kill, in the name of "justice, " Jim Nolan and Percy Munn, the protagonists of the respective novels.

Although history is used as a background for the action in the two novels, the prime consideration for both
Steinbeck and Warren is the influence of these historical
events or eras upon the two protagonists. [5] Considered in
this light, the novels are studies about what happens to people when they stop functioning as self-governing individuals
and start merging into the corporate identity of the group.
This is obviously a psychological or ecological problem rather
than a historical one.   Both Jim Nolan and Percy Munn are
young men looking for direction and meaning in their lives.
They think they find both in seemingly humanitarian causes
that fight for the rights of the proletariat. In the emotion-
charged atmosphere created by the struggle to achieve this
justice, the protagonists frequently do feel an elation of
spirit and a certainty and cleanness of purpose.   For example, shortly before he is killed, Jim's face is "transfigured.
A furious light of energy seemed to shine from it" (341).
Likewise, for a moment after the "night riders" have dyna-

mited a warehouse in which the Trust had stored its tobacco,
Percy feels a "reeling moment of certainty and fulfillment
when the air had swollen ripely with the blast" (365).

Both Jim and Percy are idealists who come to consider their adopted causes to be so essential to the ultimate
betterment of mankind that they are eventually willing to
make any sacrifice for the group goal. So befogged by the
dream of victory, they even justify acts that go against their
reason and personal ethics. Thus, Jim and Percy renounce
their individual natures by accepting the theory that good can
come from evil, that the "end" justifies the "means." In
this way they break the "magnetic chain of being" that links
them with mankind. Herein lies, say Steinbeck and Warren,
the fatal seed of the corruption and disintegration of all sensitive human beings. Both men become through their in-
creased involvement with their causes, guilty of the rational
and calculated exploitation and destruction of individual human
beings for the advancement of an abstract cause.

As men dedicated to the group goal, Percy, Jim and
Mac can justify "using" people like inanimate tools. "There's
an end to be gained ... a real end, " says Mac. "I can't
take time to think about the feelings of one man ... I'm too
busy with bunches of men" (201). With this philosophy deeply rooted in his mind, Mac teaches Jim how to use, to their
advantage, whatever opportunity comes along. Early in the
novel Mac risks a young girl's life by pretending he has had
hospital experience in delivering children. After the successful delivery, he confesses to Jim:

> I never learned till now. I never saw one before....
> That was a lucky break. We simply had to take
> it. 'Course it was nice to help the girl, but hell,
> even if it killed her--we've got to use anything
> [60].

In Night Rider, Percy Munn also learns to consider
the individual as insignificant in relation to the all-important
cause. He leads scouting parties to scrape the plant beds
of his neighbors who refuse to be pressured into joining the
Association. In vindicating himself, he uses the same reasoning that Jim and Mac adhere to. Like Jim, who must
"think only of the end" (253), Percy reflects that:

> the idea of the Association was more important
> than how he felt about [any single person]. The

idea bound a lot of men together and would get
justice for all of them. And even for men who
were not in the Association: even, in the end,
for men whose beds were scraped now [171].

Throughout both novels, Steinbeck and Warren stress
the importance of maintaining one's alter ego, one's link
with his fellow human. Steinbeck's Jim Nolan, for instance,
unfortunately loses this link for the sake of the Party and
consequently becomes insensitive to suffering. In the midst
of a violent raid on "scab" fruit pickers, Jim, feeling no
emotion at all, looks "coldly" at a fruit checker who has
just been kicked in the groin. With equal detachment he
views "ten moaning men on the ground, their faces kicked
shapeless" (180). Even Mac, Jim's hard-boiled teacher, is
frightened by the change in him. He says, "You're getting
beyond me, Jim.... I've seen men like you before. I'm
scared of 'em.... God Almighty, Jim, it's not human. I'm
scared of you" (274). In a similar manner the "night riders"
force Percy Munn into alienation, brutality, and the loss of
this "link" with humanity. Percy loses all of his capacity
to show or even to feel love, compassion, and tenderness.
He attacks his wife May and sadistically rapes her because
he is unconsciously frustrated by his self-imposed alienation.
He loses his ability to show normal affection for her or even
to talk to her (205-206). Later, after May leaves him, he
literally destroys his good friend Bill Christian by having a
meaningless affair with Christian's daughter Lucille. Even
Lucille calls Percy cold and unfeeling: "Whatever you did
[i. e. , kill a man], you did because you were cold, because
you wanted to be warm" (144). In a last attempt to regain
his self-identity, Percy tries to kill his father image and
alter ego, Senator Tolliver. He cannot do it, however, because he realizes that Tolliver is "nothing" just like himself, and "to kill a 'nothing' would prove nothing" (456).

An emphasis on the "group" and the "mass movement" is evident in both In Dubious Battle and Night Rider.
Steinbeck and Warren realize that a group is a complex entity; they try, especially Steinbeck, to explain the function
and motivation of collective action. Steinbeck defines what
he calls "group-man" as a collection of individuals who gather in periods of great tension and function with enormous
strength as a single organism. 6 In the two novels the organized groups of striking workers represent a unification of
ineffectual personal complaints into powerful action blocks
that fight for common goals. There is strength in their

definition of purpose. This group solidarity is also the
strongest and the only weapon the fruit pickers and tobacco
planters have.

In another sense, however, the group-man in these
two novels is a creature of violence; he is formed by violence and produces violence. In Steinbeck's novel, most of
the comments on violence and its inherent evil come from
Doc Burton, a self-proclaimed objective thinker who wants
to "see the whole picture" as clearly as he can without putting on the "blinders of 'good' and 'bad'" which he says
would "limit my vision" (143). Burton senses that "the end
is never very different in its nature from the means" and
asserts that one "can only build a violent thing with violence"
(253). He also philosophizes on the reasons for forming action groups and proclaims: "The group doesn't care about
the Holy Land, or Democracy, or Communism. Maybe the
group simply wants to move, to fight..." (145). This means
that although individual group members rationalize and pro-
fess that they want economic security and social justice, the
group as an entity wants nothing more than to be violent.
Mac helps to substantiate Doc Burton's thesis by constantly
insisting that only blood will raise the group's spirits and
will excite them to action. He even displays to the workers
the mutilated bodies of Joy and Jim "to step our guys up, to
keep 'em together ... [to] make 'em fight" (164). "What
they need is blood, " he cries. "A mob's got to kill something" (310).

In Night Rider, Captain Todd, Warren's "man of
principle, " also senses that justice cannot emerge from violence. He leaves the association because "the board isn't
running [it] any more. The night riders are running it"
(178). Even Dr. MacDonald, a "commander" in the "night
riders, " is not blind to the evil ingrained in the violence
that he has helped to create. When the board of the Association "sells out" to the Tobacco Trust and the "cause" is
finally lost, he tells Percy that "the reason for things is
gone" (356). Both MacDonald and Munn, as well as the rest
of the "night riders" who have scraped plant beds and destroyed warehouses, are left with the psychological and legal
consequences of their acts. Because of their defeat, they
cannot be heroes of the people whose violence may be justified through victory, but must be martyrs for their respective causes and, for MacDonald and Munn, fugitives from the
justice of the victors.

A perplexing question arises from both In Dubious Battle and Night Rider that concerns protest and its diverse ramifications. It is obviously essential that some form of protest, either violent or nonviolent, must necessarily transpire in order for justice to prevail. Because of the absence of editorial comment in the two books, however, the reader is left in doubt as to what method or methods of "battle" the authors are advocating. Violence can be ruled out at once, for Steinbeck and Warren make clear through the disastrous conclusions of both novels that desirable results cannot ensue from the demoralizing and dehumanizing brutality exhibited by the protagonists and their followers. Both authors indirectly assert that no battles can be more important than a man's personal integrity; the primacy of human dignity is clearly insisted upon. Indeed, one gets the feeling that Steinbeck and Warren are hinting at or groping toward some humane, nonviolent means of action that the oppressed workers can utilize without degrading their causes. Certainly the opposite system of emotional attacks and vindictive reprisals prove both self-destructive and self-defeating.

By now some of the parallels between In Dubious Battle and Night Rider should be clearly perceptible. We have seen that both works are novels of protest with strong historical themes and that both the tobacco planters and the fruit pickers use group violence unsuccessfully in striving to achieve their ends. Both protagonists are dehumanized through their complete devotion to the "cause." Also, both novels have much objective distance in that, although they present their causes sympathetically, neither Steinbeck nor Warren wishes to invoke compassion for his hero. And finally, in a sense, neither novel has an ending even though both plots are somewhat resolved through defeat and death. Although the lives of Jim and Percy are abruptly terminated, the mass movements they represent will undoubtedly continue forever in one form or another; the zealous feelings that give birth to group movements will prevail as long as men are exploited and humiliated.

Notes

1. Most of Steinbeck's early works, such as The Pastures of Heaven (1932), To A God Unknown (1933), Tortilla Flat (1935), In Dubious Battle (1936), Of Mice and Men (1937), The Long Valley (1938), and The Grapes of Wrath (1939), take place in central California.

Warren's Night Rider (1939), The Cave (1959); Flood:
A Romance of Our Time (1964), and many of the
short stories in The Circus in the Attic anthology
are set in the southern Kentucky-northern Tennessee
area.   For an excellent article on Warren's association with the "Southern regionalists" or "agrarians,"
see Irene Hendry, "The Regional Novel: The Example
of Robert Penn Warren," Sewanee Review,   52 (Winter,
1945),   84-102.

2. John Steinbeck, In Dubious Battle (New York: The Modern Library, 1936), p. 281. All further citations
from In Dubious Battle refer to this edition; subsequent page references are within parentheses in the
text.

3. Robert Penn Warren, Night Rider (New York: Random
House, 1939), p. 248. All further citations from
Night Rider refer to this edition; subsequent page
references are within parentheses in the text.

4. Steinbeck repeatedly asserts in his personal letters that
In Dubious Battle was not meant to be a piece of
Communist propaganda.   He declares that he was
concerned with neither Communists nor capitalists,
but only with human beings.   See Peter Lisca's The
Wide World of John Steinbeck (New Brunswick, New
Jersey: Rutgers University Press, 1958), pp. 108-
129.

5. In his book The Social Novel at the End of an Era (Carbondale, Illinois: Southern Illinois University Press,
1966), Warren French considers In Dubious Battle
and Night Rider to be "social novels" in that the authors touch upon historical events "only enough to
show how they affected the individuals whose motiva-
tions and actions most concerned them" (186).

6. This is only one aspect of Steinbeck's group-man or
"phalanx" theory.   The most complete explanation of
this theory can be found in Sea of Cortez (1941) where
group-man is defined through analogies with marine
life.

11. STEINBECK AND EMILE ZOLA

Steinbeck and Zola:
Theory and Practice of the Experimental Novel
by Lawrence William Jones

Similarities between the somewhat static, dogmatic criticism of Emile Zola's essay "The Experimental Novel" and the often biologically-oriented novels of John Steinbeck have rarely been alluded to, and certainly never really examined. Perhaps this is because the famous essay is now taken to be the statement of a too-extreme position; or perhaps because Steinbeck's critics have become so obsessed with his "decline" as a writer or the purely "social" dimensions of his work that they are willing to by-pass a careful analysis of the biological core of the novels. Whatever the case, I believe there is something to be gained from such a comparison: an insight into the relationship between scientific and literary theory.

In the first place, there is Zola's view of the novelist as experimenter, as opposed to mere observer; he said (quoting from the Introduction à l'Étude de la Médecine Expérimentale by Claude Bernard, as he does throughout):

> The name of 'observer' is given to him who applies the simple or complex process of investigation in the study of phenomena which he does not vary, and which he gathers, consequently, as nature offers them to him; the name of "experimentalist" is given to him who employs the simple and complex process of investigation to vary or modify, for an end of some kind, the natural phenomena, and to make them appear under circumstances and conditions in which they are not presented by nature. [1]

"The experimentalist," he added, "is a man who ... institutes an experiment in such a way that, in all probability,

138

it will furnish a result which will serve to confirm the hypothesis or preconceived ideas" (7).

The fact that Steinbeck is an "experimentalist" in these terms is obvious from even the most cursory glance at the bulk of his fiction--although the nature of his pre- and post-war experiments is very different. He investigates with the purpose of varying the natural phenomena by placing his characters under situational stress and describing the inevitable results. Lenny and George, for example, are under the stress of temptation from Curley's wife in Of Mice and Men, and it leads to their ultimate disaster; the families in The Pastures of Heaven are under the stress provided by the Munroes and their "evil cloud"; Mac and Jim are under the typical management-labor stress in In Dubious Battle; and the Okies of his most famous novel are of course under stress and strain from all sides. None of these are really "natural" conditions, but conditions artistically modified for the novelist's purposes. Steinbeck has in fact admitted such experimentation[2]; we have no reason to doubt it. The Salinas Valley became, in many ways, his private and miniature laboratory.

The naturalistic novelist's experiment, continued Zola, is "the offspring of the doubt which seizes him in the presence of truths little known and phenomena unexplained" (13). Writing in his "Rationale," Steinbeck indicated as much: "It is possible," he declared, "that I was trying to explain something--something that was not clear to me. I may have felt that writing it would make me understand it better."[3] He was searching, he said later in Travels with Charley, for the "small diagnostic truths which are the foundations of the larger truth,"[4] and so he experimented with fictional form as well as ideas. He always considered curiosity as one of his key traits as an artist[5] and one of the most necessary traits of human beings[6]; his overpowering, almost child-like curiosity spawned not only the fiction but a whole gamut of journalistic endeavors as well. He always possessed a great respect for what he termed in 1951 "the two great foundations of art and science: curiosity and criticism."[7]

A second most important Zolaian tenet which echoes through Steinbeck's work is that concerning "surroundings" and "heredity" and the influence òf these in society. Of the first Zola said:

... in the study of a family, of a group of living

beings, I think that the social condition is of equal
importance [to the interorganic conditions described
by Bernard].... Man is not alone; he lives in society, in a social condition; and consequently, for
us novelists, this social condition increasingly
modifies the phenomena. Indeed the great study
is just there, in the reciprocal effect of society
on the individual and the individual on society [20].

This view of the "reciprocal effect" ties in with one of Steinbeck's core notions--that of "group-man. " Steinbeck is concerned, especially in In Dubious Battle and The Grapes of
Wrath, with the social-individual relationship and tends to
see it, at this stage in his career, in animal terms. He
thus equates "social" conditions with "ecological" conditions;
in The Sea of Cortez and Cannery Row (even though the
former is not a fictional demonstration of the idea) he sees
the tide pool as a perfect microcosm of human life. This
animal analogy, though, does not detract from the emphasis
Steinbeck places on Zola's "reciprocal effect. " Steinbeck
takes man from the hands of the ecologists (who had themselves already made the transition from animal to human
society) for the same reason Zola takes him (he admits)
from the hands of the physiologist: "in order to continue
the solution of how men behave when they are in society"
(20).

Tied in with this is Zola's notion of a "social circu-
lus" which he called "a solidarity ... which unites the different members and the different organisms in such a way that
if one organ becomes rotten many others are tainted and a
very complicated disease results" (28). This reminds me
of the statement in The Log from the Sea of Cortez where
Steinbeck outlines "one diagnostic trait of 'Homo Sapiens'
that groups of individuals are periodically infected with a
feverish nervousness which causes the individual to turn on
and destroy, not only his own kind, but the works of his
own kind, "8 and of the comment by Doctor Burton in In
Dubious Battle that "group-men are always getting some
kind of infection. "9 Furthermore, the complicated disease
of the latter novel has remarkable similarities to that of
Zola's own Germinal--both deal with a strike seen as an
infection and emphasize the hopelessness of any "cure. "

Although Zola touched only briefly on the question of
heredity ("I consider that the question of heredity has a
great influence in the intellectual and passionate manifesta-

tions of men, " he said [p. 19]), in actual fact heredity in
its many facets was the guiding light of his Rougon-Marquart
series; as Charles Child Walcutt pointed out, "the whole
work is conceived as tracing certain hereditary powers and
maladies through a family that spreads into every social and
professional level of the Second Empire of France. "[10] Steinbeck's version of heredity, like many of his ideas about life,
is group-oriented. Thus he speaks of "group-memory"
when discussing the Indians of the coastal regions of Mexico
in The Log from the Sea of Cortez: "Sometimes we asked
of the Indians the local names of animals we had taken, and
then they consulted together. They seemed to live on remembered things, to be so related to the seashore and the
rocky hills ... that they are these things. "[11] This concept
of group heredity is certainly given powerful fictional trans-
lation in Steinbeck's characterization of the Joad grandparents
and others in The Grapes of Wrath and again in Steinbeck's
portrayal of the closely-knit Indian community in his post-
war parable The Pearl. Something similar may be seen in
Steinbeck's depiction of the Hawley ancestry in The Winter
of Our Discontent.

A third, and perhaps the most outstanding, similarity
between Zolaian criticism and Steinbeck's work can perhaps
best be illustrated by two parallel quotes. First Zola said:

> we shall always be ignorant of the 'why' of things;
> we can only know the 'how'.... The nature of
> our minds urges us to seek the essence of the
> 'why' of things ... experiment soon teaches us
> that we must not go beyond the 'how' [22].

And then here is Steinbeck in The Log from the Sea of Cortez:

> Nonteleological thinking concerns itself primarily
> not with what should be, or could be, or might be,
> but rather with what actually 'is' --attempting at
> most to answer the already difficult questions of
> what or how, instead of why. [12]

Both writers, in other words, have the experimenter's interest in "what is" and "what happens" and avoid asking
further questions: Zola avoids this because it is properly
outside the scope of the determinism of the experimental
novel; Steinbeck avoids it for the reason that "once that
[i. e. , the nonteleological view] has been accomplished, the

'why' of it ... seems no longer preponderantly important."13

    One further interesting comparison concerns the inability of either Zola or Steinbeck to live up to the extreme demands Zola would put on the naturalistic novelist. In "The Experimental Novel," Zola expressed thus his conviction of the superiority of the natural over what he terms the "ideal":

> We naturalistic novelists submit each fact to the
> test of observation and experiment, while the
> idealistic writers admit mysterious elements which
> escape analysis.... This question of the ideal,
> from the scientific point of view, reduces itself
> to a question of indeterminates.... I dub those
> idealists who take refuge in the unknown for the
> pleasure of being there, who have a taste for the
> most risky hypothesis [36-37].

The essential absurdity of this statement is attested to by the failure of either writer to hold to it. Zola's failure, it seems, was somewhat of a paradox; for in attempting to make his Rougon-Macquart series hyper-naturalistic, in the effort to trace an uninterrupted flow of causes and effects, he was forced to stretch the truth and fashion an almost mystical hereditary pattern. Steinbeck's failure to live up to the demands of the observer-experimenter also came unconsciously; as Woodburn Ross has pointed out, "Steinbeck has developed ideas about the unity of the cosmos which may fairly be called 'mystical,' ideas which, of course, go considerably beyond what his scientific naturalism would support ... he cannot rest content with the naturalist's world of sense experience."14 Lester Jay Marks, in the most recent study of Steinbeck's work, 15 claims that this is in fact one of the best things about the fiction--that the author is able to go a step beyond naturalism and effect a kind of fusion of the worlds of biology and spirit.

    In addition, Zola professed disdain for the prophets who were always trying "to serve up nature with a strange religious and philosophical sauce, to hold fact to metaphysical man":

> The metaphysical man is dead ... the experimental
> method in letters is in the way to explain the natu-
> ral phenomena, both individual and social, or which
> metaphysicians, until now, have given only irration-

al and supernatural explanations [54].

Again, paradoxically, Zola did not realize that science itself
could become a religion; "no mystic of the Middle Ages,"
says Fredrick Greene, "had such faith in his religion as
Zola had in science"16; Darwin, Comte, Lucas and others
became the gods of a religic-scientific creed which is still
very much with us in the twentieth century. Steinbeck, on
the other hand, never explicitly maintained that metaphysical
man was dead. In the early novels, such as To A God Unknown, man's worship of the holiness of nature makes him a
religious, a metaphysical being--this much is surely implicit
in Joseph Wayne's sacrificial death atop the altar-like rock
at the novel's end. For Steinbeck, the scientific, experimental guidelines were not limiting in any way; he was taken
beyond them by his own intuition and that of his characters.

Finally, there is Zola's stipulation about the impersonality of the naturalistic novelist:

> the personal feeling of the artist is always subject
> to the higher law of truth and nature ... the per-
> sonality of the writer should only appear in the
> idea a priori and in the form [51].

Once he finds the "true observation" the artist should "disappear, or rather transform himself instantly into the observer" (7). This brings into focus one of the central problems
of the naturalistic novelist--that of achieving objectivity.
Steinbeck surely fulfills the latter part of Zola's stricture:
his personality is stamped indelibly upon both the ideas
(group-man, the "great big soul" concept, the ethical motif
of unity-separation)17 and the form of the fiction. (As I
have pointed out elsewhere, the objectivity implied in Steinbeck's "nonteleology" became a literary modus operandi in
the later fiction, where it issued in the genre of parable.)18
But in the matter of feelings Steinbeck is the direct antithe-
sis of Zola's naturalistic novelist. He is, as Woodburn Ross
puts it, "outside the strict, scientific, natural tradition" in
that he "loves whatever he considers to be 'natural'; he loves
'natural behavior. '"19 Steinbeck's feelings led him to accept
characters who were obedient to the natural "law" of group
life and those who, while living such a life, then demonstrated the virtues of altruism. Such a character is Doc of
Sweet Thursday, seen in his relationship to his work at the
tide pools but also in his forbearing, amazingly Christian relationships to those around him on Cannery Row.

In like manner, Zola himself failed to achieve the strict objectivity which true naturalism demands. Although Germinal "is a great proletarian novel, one of the most tremendous and searching novels of the century ... it has nothing to do with the hereditary laws which it is said to exemplify and establish."[20] Zola, too, became immersed in the "cause" of the novel and, in spite of the mountainous accumulation of detail, associated with it.

Although the literary theory of "The Experimental Novel" is naive, and the attempt to draw a parallel between literary and medical methodology tenuous if not absurd, it is valuable in that it demonstrates the penultimate point to which scientific naturalism in literature may come. Both Steinbeck and Zola try to pass this point and still be consistent, which neither can do. Whether Steinbeck in fact learned from Zola's example is a more difficult thing to ascertain (for many influences upon him have yet to be investigated and explained)--but surely the similarities already outlined between Zola's theory and Steinbeck's fiction suggest such a possibility.

Notes

1. Emile Zola, The Experimental Novel and Other Essays (New York, 1893), p. 6. All references are to this volume, and are included after each quotation in the text.

2. See "Critics, Critics, Burning Bright, " in Steinbeck and His Critics, ed. E. W. Tedlock, Jr. and C. V. Wicker (Albuquerque, 1957), p. 47, and Journal of a Novel (New York, 1969), pp. 6, 8. The actual process of experimentation by the author is discussed in an essay by the late Horace P. Taylor, Jr., "Steinbeck--The Quest, " McNeese Review, 16 (1965), 41 and passim.

3. Tedlock and Wicker, p. 309.

4. Travels with Charley (New York, 1961), p. 5.

5. Ibid., pp. 116-117.

6. "Let's Go After the Neglected Treasures Beneath the Seas, " Popular Science, 189 (September, 1966), 85.

7. *Journal of a Novel*, p. 15. For a summary of other
    statements Steinbeck makes about his own art in this
    volume, see my review in *Saturday Review*, 52 (De-
    cember 20, 1969), 25-26.

8. *The Log from the Sea of Cortez* (New York, 1951), pp.
    16-17.

9. *In Dubious Battle* (New York, 1936), p. 104.

10. *American Literary Naturalism: A Divided Stream* (Min-
    neapolis, 1956), p. 23.

11. Tedlock and Wicker, p. 211.

12. *Sea of Cortez*, p. 135.

13. *Ibid.*, p. 146.

14. Woodburn O. Ross in Tedlock and Wicker, p. 210.

15. *Thematic Design in the Novels of John Steinbeck* (The
    Hague, 1969), pp. 22-23.

16. *French Novelists from the Revolution to Proust* (New
    York, 1931), p. 278.

17. The group-man concept is best treated in an unpublished
    doctoral dissertation (Louisiana State, 1961) by Ho-
    race Platt Taylor, Jr.; mystical ideas are treated in
    several essays in Tedlock and Wicker; essays by
    Gibbs and Kennedy in Tedlock and Wicker treat ethi-
    cal notions in Steinbeck's work.

18. See "A Little Play in Your Head: Parable Form in
    John Steinbeck's Post-War Fiction," *Genre*, 3 (March
    1970), 55-63. It is interesting to note that Zola con-
    siders the true naturalistic novelist to be also an "ex-
    perimental moralist," to be one of the "most moral
    workers in the human workshop" (25-26). This he
    predicates on the ground that such a novelist can best
    objectively view the human passions and values in any
    given situation. The fact that Steinbeck considers
    himself an "experimental moralist" in this sense is
    perhaps obvious from his approach to the Nazi-Nor-
    wegian struggle in *The Moon Is Down*; in the pre-war
    work his "staged" narrative often makes moral judg-

ment seem out of place, as in <u>Of Mice and Men</u>, but in most of the post-war books Steinbeck found it impossible to stand aside from the moral conflict, often making it much too clear where <u>he</u> stood in relation to the issue involved--this is particularly true of <u>East of Eden</u> and <u>The Winter of Our Discontent.</u>

19.   Woodburn O. Ross in Tedlock and Wicker, pp. 208-209.

20.   Walcutt, p. 37.

Part II

CRITICISM AND BIBLIOGRAPHY

1. A SURVEY OF STEINBECK CRITICISM, TO 1971[1]

by Peter Lisca

When the first serious criticism of Steinbeck's work
began to appear at the end of the Depression decade, he was
thirty-seven years old and had been publishing steadily for
ten years--seven novels, two books of short stories (of
which five had appeared in the North American Review, two
in Harper's Magazine and one in the Atlantic Monthly), an
article in The Nation, and a series of seven articles in the
San Francisco News. In this respect his experience is similar to that of William Faulkner, who waited about the same
period for recognition. Although the spectacle of all those
promising, young American writers who disappear after rave
reviews and motion picture production of their first novel
(followed by a series of television appearances) makes early
neglect seem a benevolent influence, for a writer of various
capacities and directions such neglect may have a malign effect. Belated discovery can establish a conception of the
writer's style and subject matter which, although usually
based only upon his most recent work, becomes extended
by careless critics and rapid reviewers as the basis for
understanding not only his earlier work but even work not
yet written.

For Steinbeck, the critical stereotype was founded on
the three novels appearing in rapid succession at the end of
the 1930's--In Dubious Battle, Of Mice and Men, and The
Grapes of Wrath. It did not matter that of his previous fiction, all published during the same decade of the Great Depression, none of the novels and only one of the short stories
had dealt with current themes--political, social, economic--
or were even in current settings. As Faulkner's work was
subsumed under the critical stereotype of "Southern Gothic,"
so Steinbeck's work was supposed to be "Proletarian" and
"Naturalistic." Thus it was possible to look back and see
that Cup of Gold exemplified the defeat of materialism, and
that To A God Unknown and Tortilla Flat did not properly
belong in the Steinbeck canon at all because they did not

seem to embody what were assumed, or expected to be, the
author's social sympathies. As late as 1947, the Time re-
viewer of The Wayward Bus could see clearly that in this
novel "each of Steinbeck's principal characters may be dimly
identified with a stock role in a leftist parable. " Ironically,
it was largely on the basis of this stereotype simplification
of his work that between 1939 and 1941 Steinbeck reached
the first peak of his reputation--an eminence from which he
declined steadily, with but a brief resurgence in the early
1950's (East of Eden) until his beginning rise again in the
1960's.

At the height of this first peak in his critical reputation it was Steinbeck, not Hemingway, Fitzgerald, Dos Passos, or Faulkner, who was considered both at home and
abroad as the American writer from whom the most was to
be expected in the future. Where this high expectation was
doubted or qualified, that doubt focused not on the question
of Steinbeck's ability to utilize with equal effectiveness post-
Depression materials but rather on what were assumed to be
inherent weaknesses of technique. In his America in Contemporary Fiction, Percy Boynton stated that "California and
Oklahoma, peach and cotton picking, are incidental to Steinbeck. What he is concerned with are the human hungers for
food, for joy, for security. "[2] On the other hand, his variety
of prose styles and organizing structures (The Pastures of
Heaven, Tortilla Flat, In Dubious Battle) was seen not as
evidence of the author's fertility of imagination but as attempts to find "the right artistic medium" for what he had
to say--as if Steinbeck were supposed to have only one thing
to say and there were of course only one way to say it.
Few critics, however, doubted that Steinbeck's star was just
rising on the literary horizon.

Although dating from this first period of enthusiasm,
the first study of Steinbeck in book form was very well balanced and perceptive. In addition to a check list of first
editions and a biographical sketch prepared with the aid of
his subject, Harry T. Moore's volume, The Novels of John
Steinbeck, contained sixty-odd pages of analysis devoid of
critical and political hobby-horses. In chronological order
he examined each of the seven novels, concentrating on whatever aspects of form and content seemed significant in each,
yet not neglecting to note the development or persistence of
certain pervasive interests from one novel to another--such
as the group-protagonist, the biological metaphor, and the
extensive use of myth and legend. In addition, although

Moore had great praise for some aspects of Steinbeck's art, he did not hesitate to point out certain weaknesses. Although liable to the inherent inadequacies of a pioneer study, this slim volume written in 1939 contains many insights which have been elaborated by subsequent serious criticism.

Unfortunately, the valuable influence of Moore's book was not immediately felt and it was not until almost twenty years later that criticism returned to these directions.   Instead, critics found it much easier to repeat certain erroneous conclusions which Edmund Wilson had first published in an essay, "The Californians: Storm and Steinbeck" and reprinted in two popular collections of his essays.   It was not that Wilson's conclusions were original, but that they were voiced in memorable phrases by a respected and influential commentator on the literary scene.   Thus, Wilson's conclusion (based on an admittedly incomplete knowledge of Steinbeck's work) that "Mr. Steinbeck almost always in his fiction is dealing either with the lower animals or with human beings so rudimentary that they are almost on the animal level" finds frequent repetition in subsequent studies.   Elizabeth N. Monroe, Alfred Kazin, Stanley Edgar Hyman, Max Eastman, Maxwell Geismar, Freeman Champney, and Frederick J. Hoffman, among many others, found occasion to note that Steinbeck "habitually and characteristically sets human conduct and animal conduct side by side," that Steinbeck is "much more interested in the natural scene, and in animal life, than in people or the human emotions of his narratives," that Steinbeck's failure to give "a convincing definition of his people" was caused by his having "reduced the scale of definition to their animal nature," that Steinbeck's characters are "animated by the simpler forms of protoplasmic irritability," etc., ad nauseum.   In these studies Wilson's essay is frequently quoted.   And this influence persisted, despite some dozen subsequent studies more comprehensive and precise, until the 1960's.

Two of these influential critics, Hyman and Geismar, elaborated further inadequate hypotheses about Steinbeck's work.   Starting from the acceptable proposition that Steinbeck's work swings between extremes in its depiction of the individual's relationship to society, Hyman proceeds to make this relationship the central theme of every novel.   Further, by confounding Steinbeck with his characters he can arrive at such conclusions as that in Cup of Gold the author is espousing an individualistic philosophy, that in The Pastures of Heaven he is proving Nature good and Man evil, and finally that in In Dubious Battle Steinbeck has embraced Communism. Geismar, like Wilson, saw the variety and flexibility of the work as indications of weakness, a frustrated search for values in which Steinbeck "seems about to traverse the entire circuit of contemporary escapes. In him are reflected the evasions of his generation. " This after In Dubious Battle and The Grapes of Wrath!

Beginning with Frederick I. Carpenter's "The Philosophical Joads, " there appeared in the 1940's a series of essays devoted to The Grapes of Wrath which did much to focus attention on the native intellectual currents in that novel. Carpenter's convincing demonstration that Steinbeck's "proletarian" novel was in the stream of such American thinkers as Emerson, Whitman, and William James was carried further by Chester Eisinger in his essay, "Jeffersonian Agrarianism in The Grapes of Wrath. " In his American Idealism, Floyd Stovall also had seen Steinbeck securely in the mainstream of American thought. Just how far the reading public was out of touch with these traditions could be inferred from Martin Staples Shockley's documentation of "The Reception of The Grapes of Wrath in Oklahoma. " Differing markedly from these attempts to understand Steinbeck's works in sociological or historical terms was Woodburn Ross's essay "John Steinbeck: Earth and Stars. " Ross saw Steinbeck as "a man of two worlds"--the world of science, and the world of "affections and intuitions. " Steinbeck is, therefore, "at the same time brutal and tender, rational and irrational, concrete and abstract. His imagination provides for humanity a home in the universe which his senses do not perceive. " Viable as this thesis may be, however, Ross was not able to take it much beyond its simple statement without running into such a serious contradiction as to conclude that in Steinbeck everything which is "natural" is good.

Those studies of Steinbeck's work which were more or less esthetically oriented were few. Perhaps the best of these were Joseph Warren Beach's two chapters on Steinbeck in his American Fiction, 1920-1940, especially the chapter on The Grapes of Wrath, which novel he thought "perhaps the finest example so far produced in the United States of the proletarian novel. " His observations on the unity of the narrative with the inter-chapters and his rationale for the effectiveness and credibility of the characters was especially valuable. On this latter point Beach was to find himself in disagreement with two heirs of Edmund Wilson's pronouncements--Alfred Kazin and W. M. Frohock. "Steinbeck's peo-

ple, " said Kazin in On Native Grounds, "are always on the
verge of becoming human but never do, " thus allowing the
author to slip into "calculated sentimentality. " Frohock, in
"John Steinbeck's Men of Wrath" was so insensitive as to
assert that "the people of The Grapes of Wrath and In Dubious Battle are essentially the people of Tortilla Flat and
Cannery Row, " and so illogical as to say on the heels of
this that The Grapes of Wrath is a good tragedy because
there "his people have the requisite human dignity. " Whereas Barker Fairley in "John Steinbeck and the Coming Literature" saw a direct relationship between Steinbeck's reliance
on the working man's speech and the excellence of his fiction, and, similarly, Lincoln Gibbs, while objecting to Steinbeck's free treatment of sex, approved of his writings because they "make for democracy, " Norman Cousins in "Who
Are the Real People?" objected that it should be "at least
possible to write about the mainstream of humanity without
putting a halo on the half-wit, deifying the drunk, or canon-
izing the castoff. "

Ironically, one of the most valuable essays to appear
in this period between Sea of Cortez and The Wayward Bus
was a noncritical piece of work by Lewis Gannett called
"John Steinbeck: Novelist at Work. " Mr. Gannett merely
presented, in chronological order, selections from Steinbeck's
correspondence with his agents over a period of fourteen
years. In these letters discussing his tentative plans for
the novels, his problems in realizing them, the purposes
of his writing, and other such significant matters, lay convincing proof that, whatever his failures or accomplishments,
Steinbeck's motives were apolitical, humanistic, esthetic,
and that his integrity was uncompromised. These were
particularly important points to establish, as much of the
criticism had been based on erroneous assumptions concerning the author's intentions.

It may be concluded generally that while a good deal
of the criticism between 1941 and 1947 was unfavorable, it
was nevertheless concerned. The two books of fiction published in these years, The Moon is Down and Cannery Row,
were not up to the expectations raised by Of Mice and Men
and The Grapes of Wrath, but the feeling was that the author
who had promised so much in these earlier works, fraught
with lapses of taste and philosophy though they were, might
yet come through with something.

It is instructive to compare this spirit of watchful

waiting with Steinbeck's growing reputation in Europe, particularly France, which in the past had discovered for us some of our leading writers and was currently introducing us to William Faulkner. Mme. Vaucher-Zananiri's book, Voix d'Amerique: Études sur la littérature américaine d'aujourd'hui, devoted as much space to the work of Steinbeck as to Hemingway, Faulkner, and Dos Passos combined, finding it to be "without doubt one of the more significant and important among those of contemporary American writers."[3] Qualifying and particularizing such high praise, this critic continued: "I do not believe that Steinbeck is actually the best writer on the other side of the Atlantic. Faulkner or even Hemingway have attained summits he is incapable of ascending. But he is unquestionably the most complete and human. "

Whereas American critics were concerned with Steinbeck's sentimentalism and animalism, French critics were more concerned with trying to discover the basic premises of his art and attempting to define his style. For Maurice Coindreau ("Quadrille américain": Les Oeuvres nouvelles) Steinbeck's art was primarily that of

> a romantic and a poet of acute sensitivity, profoundly idealist. Of this sensitivity is born the desire for escape which, in various guises, stirs all of his characters. All dream, and the end of these dreams is always a disillusion.

Another critic, Jean Blanzat, proposed a very different thesis in his article, "John Steinbeck: Romancier de la fatalité," in which he compared Steinbeck's sense of tragedy to that of Sophocles:

> Neither Hemingway, more cosmopolitan and more diverse, nor Faulkner, more complex and singular, are in this respect as significant as John Steinbeck. With Steinbeck for the first time perhaps the recent art of the novel rejoins not the themes but the spirit of Greek tragedy.

This critic's essay is interesting also for its attention to Steinbeck's réalisme, which is found to be more an effect of its basis in archetype and myth than of its surface detail. In another French essay on this topic, "Le Réalisme lyrique de John Steinbeck, " René Lalou analyzes the peculiar effectiveness of Steinbeck's "realistic" prose style. This effec-

tiveness, said M. Lalou, springs from Steinbeck's refusal to
renounce his privilege as a writer, "which is to enlarge un-
ceasingly our vision, to never chain it to the simple present
spectacle. " Thus Steinbeck's "intrusions" into his novels
make his "descriptive realism" pass into a "lyric realism. "

Perhaps the best of this French criticism is Claude-
Edmonde Magny's chapter on Steinbeck in her excellent book,
L'Age du roman américain. Mme. Magny called her chapter
"Steinbeck, or the Limits of the Impersonal Novel. " As the
title suggests, she was not entirely sympathetic towards
Steinbeck's works. The contribution of her study was the
new light it threw on Steinbeck's use of what T. K. Whipple,
ten years earlier, had called "the middle distance. " This
"impersonality, " as Mme. Magny calls it, is "the continental divide in his work, from which flow on the one hand his
faults and on the other his virtues. " When this "impersonality" is unsuccessful it results in characters who are less
than human--Danny, Pilon, Johnny Bear, Lennie, and the
"bad boys of Cannery Row. " On the other hand, when this
technique is successful it enables him to deal with violence
without horror, social issues without propaganda, sentiment
without sentimentality, and realism without vulgarity. In
addition, Magny pointed out that what may sometimes seem
Steinbeck's failure to create "living" characters is the result of his absorbing the characters into his materials, as
in In Dubious Battle and The Grapes of Wrath. The characters are not intended to affect us as individuals because
Steinbeck's controlling view was essentially impersonal.
Even the larger aspect of the Joad's migration is but part
of an even larger pattern with which Steinbeck is concerned.
The same is true of In Dubious Battle:

> And the true subject, the true hero of the book,
> is not the individual destiny of Mac or Jim, but
> the history of their common task, this strike of
> fruit-pickers of which the novel is the Iliad, be-
> hind which even further, we see profile itself an
> adventure more vast, more impersonal yet, of
> which it is but an episode.

Magny goes on to suggest that Mac and Jim--unlike such
characters as Dos Passos' Glenn Spotswood, "whose im-
penitent individualism too often retains our exclusive attention to the detriment of the proletarian adventure considered
as a whole"--are but "privileged observers--half actors, half
acted upon. "

With these critics writing in French should be associated also the Belgian critic Albert Gérard, who in 1947
published a forty-seven page monograph called A la rencontre
de John Steinbeck. Although Gérard agreed in part with such
American critics as Hyman and Geismar, he was able to
perceive, as they could not, such things as the structural
role of humor in Tortilla Flat, making his essay the best
study of that novel that had yet been published. His remarks
on the technique of the stories in The Long Valley were
equally excellent. He observed that they "unfold according
to a rhythm determined by the outcome; they do not content
themselves with beginning and ending: they have a beginning
and an ending. " Steinbeck chooses as the subject of his
stories "those instants in which the convergence of the living being and the outcome results in the creation of a story
and a character at one and the same time. " Throughout,
Gérard demonstrates an intimate knowledge of Steinbeck's
works and can comment on his use of motion picture tech-
niques in Cup of Gold, irony in The Pastures of Heaven and
esthetic distance in Of Mice and Men. The work of Gérard,
and Magny as well, must be ranked with that of Harry T.
Moore and Joseph Warren Beach. It is unfortunate that it
was not more easily available.

The American critical attitude of watchful waiting between 1941 and 1947 erupted into violent reaction with the
publication of The Wayward Bus and The Pearl. The tenor
of some essays, those by Norman Cousins, Donald Weeks,
and Ben Ray Redman, for example, can be inferred from
their titles: "Bankrupt Realism, " "The Case of John Steinbeck, " "Steinbeck Against Steinbeck. " Clearly, in 1947
Steinbeck was on trial, but the charges were confusing.
Whereas Champney insisted that the author's best field was
"the sub-rational and the inarticulate, " Geismar leveled the
charge that "of all the ranking modern writers who have
gone back to primitive materials as a protest against and
a solace for contemporary society, Steinbeck is, as a matter of fact, the least well-endowed. " Blake Nevius, on the
other hand, laid the blame for Steinbeck's decline on his increasingly "scientific" view of life.

The historians of American literature were no kinder.
Frederick J. Hoffman, in The Modern Novel in America,
found that Steinbeck's novels "reveal the deficiencies of a
homespun philosophy, in which the suggestions made are
vitiated and confused by a 'hausfrau sentimentality' and a
naive mysticism. " Orville Prescott signalled his opinion

by the title of that chapter in which he considered Sinclair
Lewis and Hemingway as well as Steinbeck--"Squandered
Talents. " In The Shapers of American Fiction, George D.
Snell thought The Grapes of Wrath "as formless a novel as
could well be, " and Of Mice and Men "a negligible novel
seemingly written with a determined eye on the cash register. "
This latter novel was seen by Wagenknecht in his Cavalcade
of the American Novel as "a glorification of idiocy, " and,
like Edwin Burgum in The Novel and the World's Dilemma
as well as Geismar and Wilson earlier, he judged Steinbeck's
"versatility" to be proof that Steinbeck could not "find" himself as a writer. Finally, in Fifty Years of the American
Novel: A Catholic Appraisal, John S. Kennedy saw Steinbeck's work as denying man "the attribute of sovereign intellect and unforced free will which alone make man more
than the beasts that perish. "

Although this period between Cannery Row (1945) and
Burning Bright (1950) saw many of the most prejudiced attacks on Steinbeck's work, it also brought forth a few pene-
trating analyses which still stand as valuable pieces of criticism. Foremost among these are two essays by Frederick
Bracher and Woodburn Ross. Interestingly, both addressed
themselves to the topic of "Steinbeck and the Biological View
of Man, " as Bracher called his essay; "John Steinbeck:
Naturalism's Priest" was the title used by Ross. Returning
to that aspect of Steinbeck's work which had occasioned the
harsh attacks by Edmund Wilson and his followers, both
Bracher and Ross saw deeper into Steinbeck's biological
metaphors. Although it is true, said Bracher, that Steinbeck has "a way of looking at things characteristic of a bi-
ologist, " unlike his ancestors in literary naturalism Steinbeck's acceptance of man's biological citizenship in the created world extends to a mystic reverence for "life in all its
forms. " For, "to be aware of the whole thing and to accept one's part in it is, for Steinbeck, the saving grace
which may lift man out of the tidepool. " Very similarly,
Ross found that Steinbeck's achievement lay "in taking the
materials which undermined the religious faith of the nineteenth century and fusing them with a religious attitude. "
Thus, "Nature as described by the scientist ... supplies ...
the basis of a sense of reverence. " He accorded Steinbeck
the distinction of being "the first significant novelist to begin to build a mystical religion upon a naturalistic base. "
Although not extendable to Steinbeck's later fiction, this view
of his work up to 1950 has come to seem very plain twenty
years later.

➡️There were also between 1945 and 1950 some pei
tive reviews of the novels published in this period. Both
Thomas Sugrue and Carlos Baker praised The Pearl for it
symbolic content, its "ubiquitous associational potential," as
Baker put it, which Sugrue detailed as an essay into "the
knowledge of spiritual growth and its rejection." Baker also
wrote a perceptive review of The Wayward Bus, in which he
remarked its "richness of texture" and "solidity of structure."

If the true barometer of a writer's critical reputation
is the frequency with which his works are analyzed in the
literary quarterlies, it may be concluded that the above excellent essays and reviews had no effect on that reputation.
The amazing fact is that between 1950 and 1955 the bibliography section of American Literature contained only three items
under Steinbeck--exactly the number appearing under Mickey
Spillane! Even of these three, two were extended book reviews, one by a French critic, Claude-Edmonde Magny; the
essay by Bernard Bowron was an exegesis of The Grapes of
Wrath which reduced that novel to a piece of "literary en-
gineering" in the genre of "Wagons West" romance. Yet, in
the following year Warren French energetically attacked this
thesis, and in 1956 Martin Staples Shockley published his
"Christian Symbolism in The Grapes of Wrath," which, although adding little to Harry T. Moore's observations, was
to become the opening gambit in a series of little skirmishes
on that topic in the pages of College English.

Thus, although by the mid-1950's, there had appeared
a handful of provocative essays on Steinbeck's work in general and some perceptive essays on individual novels, mostly
The Grapes of Wrath, except for Moore's early (1939) and
short pioneer effort, no book had yet appeared on this writer who had published fourteen novels, two volumes of short
stories, two documentary volumes, a journal of travel, and
co-authored a book-length essay on biology as philosophy;
had seen three of his novels staged on Broadway (one of
them with remarkable success, winning the New York Drama
Critics' Circle Award), and eight of them into motion pictures; and had even won a Pulitzer prize. The assumption
of critics seemed to be that this work would not support sustained critical inquiry.

Obviously, such a situation could not long endure, and
the last fifteen years have produced such a wealth of Steinbeck criticism that it is not possible here to deal with it in
the fairly detailed manner of the earlier period. The first

major breakthrough was the publication in 1957 by E. W.
Tedlock, Jr. and C. V. Wicker of Steinbeck and His Critics.
This collection of essays, all but three previously published,
included also six short items by Steinbeck himself relating
to his reception by the critics.   The first and longest essay
was one of the original pieces, my own "John Steinbeck:
A Literary Biography," which, together with the following
essay, Lewis Gannett's "John Steinbeck's Way of Writing,"
presented the fullest documentation of Steinbeck's artistic
integrity.   By bringing together the best that had been published and some original essays on the later novels this
book had a stimulating effect on future critics.   In the following year appeared the first full-length study (326 pages),
The Wide World of John Steinbeck by myself.   I had also,
in addition to three essays for Steinbeck and His Critics,
published "The Grapes of Wrath as Fiction" in PMLA,
March, 1957.   The Wide World of John Steinbeck was the
first critical study to avail itself of Steinbeck's correspondence with his agents (McIntosh & Otis) and editor (Pascal
Covici).   By utilizing this correspondence and the best of
previous criticism, and trying to avoid any sociological or
even critical disposition, this book, although sometimes pro-
voking subsequent disagreements with particular analyses or
evaluations, has remained a viable influence, as attested by
the frequence with which it is cited and its continuation in
print to the present time.

Whereas, with the exception of Moore's early book,
criticism had contented itself with essay-length attempts to
deal with Steinbeck's work as a whole, soon after The Wide
World of John Steinbeck there appeared several other book-
length studies.   The first of these was Warren French's
John Steinbeck (190 pages), published in Twayne's United
States Authors series in 1961.   This was followed in 1962
by F. W. Watt's volume (117 pages) of the same title for
Evergreen's Pilot Books, and in 1963 by Joseph Fontenrose's
John Steinbeck: An Introduction and Interpretation (150 pages),
published in the American Authors and Critics series of
Barnes and Noble.   Thus, three separate book-length studies
appeared in as many years.   Regrettably, however, although
these volumes contributed to the availability of Steinbeck material and thus stimulates still further discussion and study
of Steinbeck's work, their contribution of fresh, original material was rather limited, confining itself to a few details of
biography or the identification of locale in the fiction.   Nor,
with one exception, did they contribute substantially to new
understandings of the work.

This exception was Joseph Fontenrose's John Steinbeck: An Introduction and Interpretation. Taking up the
novels in chronological order, and almost always by apply-
ing his very considerable knowledge of folklore, myth, and
the classics (of which he was professor at Berkeley), Fontenrose frequently took up where the trail had grown cold
for previous critics and followed it through the woods of allusion and symbol as if it were a six-lane freeway. Steinbeck's Cup of Gold, for example, was found to embody not
only Faustian motifs but also Grail legends, the fall of Troy,
and aspects of Peer Gynt. And it was convincingly demonstrated that this first novel is structured on these "four in-
tertwined myths to which are subordinated several folkloris-
tic themes." Fontenrose also succeeded, where others had
failed, in finding exact and meaningful relations between Tortilla Flat and the Morte d'Arthur. Taking the title In Dubious Battle to be more than just a passing allusion, he traced
out the specific parallels to individual scenes, fallen angels,
debates in hell, and harangues by Satan, as well as the pervasive general significance of the allusion. Even in the
chapter on The Grapes of Wrath, the novel most worked
over by the critics, Fontenrose was able to extend our knowledge of that novel's religious symbols and references. Cannery Row, too, benefited from an intensive application of
this kind of knowledge. To his discussion of Sea of Cortez,
he brought a wider intellectual background than previous
critics had mustered, resulting in generalizations about
Steinbeck's world view which were critical and valid: "In
Steinbeck's novels biology takes the place of history, mysticism takes the place of humanism." Unfortunately, Fontenrose's disinclination for Steinbeck's later work, in which
he found that "myth is externally imposed on the material"
in an attempt to achieve significance, prevented him from
dealing at sufficient length with Steinbeck's work after Cannery Row.

After the above three books in quick sequence there
appeared no other critical volume for six years. But in
1967 Tetsumaro Hayashi brought out his John Steinbeck: A
Concise Bibliography. It was a work much needed. Unfortunately, it contained numerous errors of various kinds--
duplication of material under different titles, erroneous authorship, mis-identification of periodicals as books, errors
in page reference, etc. Nevertheless, despite these errors,
which are being corrected for a second edition, this work
remains an indispensable critical tool, containing almost
every scrap of relevant material. Furthermore, Hayashi's

continued interest has resulted in a cumulative supplement
(1968) and regular additions to the bibliography in the Steinbeck Quarterly.

The most recent book about John Steinbeck is Lester
Jay Marks' Thematic Design in the Novels of John Steinbeck
(144 pages), 1969. The title itself is encouraging, for surely
after four book-length general surveys of Steinbeck's work it
is time that some more particularly oriented, defined examination be undertaken. Mr. Marks' thesis is that "three thematic patterns recur consistently" throughout Steinbeck's
novels: "that man is a religious creature ..., that mankind
may also be viewed biologically, as a 'group animal' [and]
the 'non-teleological' concept that man lives without knowledge
of the cause of his existence." But these points have long
been recognized, and the book does not make as substantial
a contribution to our understanding of them as would be desirable.

Although in the last fifteen years, as duly noted in
the Hayashi bibliographies, there have appeared at least a
score of general books on American literature which find
occasion to give more than passing mention to Steinbeck's
work, these books of necessity must deal briefly with a
large subject and have not made significant contributions.
Steinbeck fares much better in those books organized around
some more specific topic. There is an interesting treatment
of Of Mice and Men in Winifred Dusenbury's The Theme of
Loneliness in Modern American Drama; Warren French ex-
plores the sociological background of The Grapes of Wrath
in his The Social Novel at the End of an Era, and he should
also be cited for his own contributions to his two collections
--A Companion to The Grapes of Wrath and American Winners
of the Nobel Prize. In Pseudonyms of Christ in the Modern
Novel, E. M. Moseley relates Jim Casy to the wider context
of Christ symbolism in the 1930's. But with few exceptions
the best work on Steinbeck, the most explorative and original
has appeared either as original contributions to special collections or in periodicals. Of particular interest among the
collections are such essays as Pascal Covici, Jr.'s "John
Steinbeck and the Language of Awareness," in Warren French's
volume, The Thirties. This essay is helpful in understanding
the failure of Steinbeck's early critics to come to meaningful
grips with his work, pointing out that in addition to Steinbeck's preoccupation with the land problems, the people, and
the social forces of the thirties there is his achievement in
presenting "the struggle of individuals toward that awareness

that is 'locked in wordlessness.'" Also interesting are H.
Paul Hunter's "Steinbeck's Wine of Affirmation," dealing
further with Christian elements in The Grapes of Wrath, in
R. E. Langford's Essays in Modern American Literature,
and the short but provocative, "'The Endless Journey to No
End,'" by Agnes McNeill Donohue in her own A Casebook on
The Grapes of Wrath (1968). Donohue points out interesting
parallels to Hawthorne's Journey and Eden symbolism.

Particular mention here should be made of two other
collections: first, the Spring, 1965, issue of Modern Fiction
Studies, which was devoted entirely to Steinbeck and which
contains some half-dozen good articles and a useful, selected
bibliography; second, Steinbeck: The Man and His Work, the
collection of papers delivered at the Steinbeck conference in
Corvallis, Oregon in April of 1970. Both these volumes
contain essays of major significance, which will be particu-
larized below.

Of those essays appearing in periodicals, it is again
true that generally the least valuable have been those which
attempt some total assessment or topical survey. "Steinbeck's
Image of Man and His Decline as a Writer" and "Steinbeck
and Hemingway: Suggestions for a Comparative Study," my
own contributions to this genre, risk this same judgment.
Richard Astro's two essays, "Steinbeck and Mainwaring:
Two Californians for the Earth," in which he emphasizes
that Steinbeck's relationship to other "proletarian" writers
of the 1930's needs examination, and his "Steinbeck's Post-
War Trilogy: A Return to Nature and the Natural Man," ex-
ploring Steinbeck's traditional view of nature and the natural
world in Cannery Row, The Wayward Bus, and The Pearl,
surely are fruitful directions for the general essay. On the
other hand, James Woodress' "John Steinbeck: Hostage to
Fortune" tells us yet again that

> Steinbeck ... is another writer who is a victim of
> his own success. ... When he was most afraid of
> popularity and monetary success, he was most the
> social critic and the best writer. When he was
> being engulfed by success, the struggle against it
> produced some excellent work. But when he was
> drowned by popularity and royalties, Steinbeck en-
> tered his period of artistic decline.

This is no more illuminating than Arthur Mizener's objections
to Steinbeck's Nobel Prize in 1962--

Perhaps the explanation is ... the time has come
around for some American to receive the award,
and among Europeans Steinbeck turned out to be,
for one or another reason, the most widely read
American author, just as Sinclair Lewis was when
he received the Nobel Prize in 1930.

Similarly, Margaret C. Roane's article on some of Steinbeck's mentally retarded minor characters may be interesting clinically, but has no literary issue. And although perhaps interesting enough for the general reader, such an article as "Steinbeck's Image of the West" by Walter Rundell,
Jr. in The American West, is of little value to the scholar
and critic. A concise though somewhat inaccurate survey
(18 pages) of Steinbeck criticism from the beginnings to 1969
is provided by Warren French in his contribution to Fifteen
Modern American Authors edited by Jackson R. Bryer.

The Corvallis volume of essays, co-edited by Richard
Astro, who was also responsible for the choice of papers
presented at the conference, and by Tetsumaro Hayashi, contains some exceptions to the general inconsequence of the
general essay. John Ditsky's comparison of "Faulkner Land
and Steinbeck Country" does much to bring these two writers,
seemingly so different, closer together. Joel Hedgpeth's examination of Steinbeck's relationship to Ed Ricketts in "Philosophy on Cannery Row" is especially valuable, providing
an approach to that relationship which will surely cause an
important re-evaluation of Ricketts' contribution to Steinbeck's writing. Charles Metzger's "Steinbeck's Mexican-
Americans" is a thorough survey of its subject. Perhaps
my own contribution to this volume, also a general essay,
"Escape and Commitment: Two Poles of the Steinbeck Hero," will also prove fruitful.

As might be expected, those essays devoting them-
selves to particular stories and novels tend to gather around
a few works and ignore others. Of the short stories, "The
Chrysanthemums," "Flight," and the stories of The Red
Pony have attracted the most attention. Among these, "The
Texts of Steinbeck's 'The Chrysanthemums,'" by William
Osborne; "The Lost Dream of Sex and Childbirth in 'The
Chrysanthemums,'" by Mordecai Marcus; "A Reading of
Steinbeck's 'Flight,'" by John Antico; and perhaps "Thematic
Rhythm in The Red Pony," by Arnold L. Goldsmith are the
most interesting. Osborne's discovery of textual variations
in the two printed versions is essential.

Of the novels, The Pearl has provided a topic for two
essays in English Journal, attesting to that novel's popularity
in high school literature courses: Bartel Roland's "Proportioning in Fiction: The Pearl and Silas Marner, " and Harry
Morris' "Realism and Allegory in The Pearl. " Morris cor-
rects some of French's dissatisfactions with that novel and
points to some precise parallels to the 14th century anonymous poem by the same name. Two full-length articles
have appeared on Tortilla Flat, but Arthur F. Kinney's "The
Arthurian Cycle in Tortilla Flat" does not seem aware of
Fontenrose's work and is thus needlessly repetitive. Likewise, "The Conflict of Form in Tortilla Flat" by Stanley
Alexander has little to recommend it. The author begins by
taking issue with passages from previous critics whom he
misinterprets and then goes on to conclude simplistically
that the novel fails because it is a mixture of two forms--
the mock-heroic and the pastoral. He makes much of this
latter mode and quotes Empson, but does not seem to have
knowledge of the excellent work done eight years earlier on
the application of Some Versions of the Pastoral to Steinbeck
--Charles Metzger's essay on Sweet Thursday, "Steinbeck's
Version of the Pastoral. " Metzger demonstrates, most interestingly, that "anyone re-reading Sweet Thursday with the
pastoral tradition in mind can recognize immediately several
of the major features discussed by Mr. Empson. " This essay, together with Robert DeMott's "Steinbeck and the Creative Process" in Steinbeck: The Man and His Work (Corvallis, 1971), have done much to cause a serious re-evaluation of that seemingly trivial novelette and its position in
Steinbeck's work. There have been two good essays on
Steinbeck's last novel, The Winter of Our Discontent. Warren French's "Steinbeck's Winter Tale" traces the novel's
origins in an earlier short story, "How Mr. Hogan Robbed
a Bank, " and points out interesting parallels to Salinger's
The Catcher in the Rye. Donna Gerstenberger's essay,
"Steinbeck's American Wasteland, " finds detailed parallels
to Eliot's poem. Unfortunately, Cannery Row, a much un-
derrated novel, has been attended by only one essay, in the
Corvallis volume.

On Steinbeck's novels of the Thirties, three short
items have appeared on Of Mice and Men, Dusenbury's essay (noted above) and Warren French's researches into "The
First Theatrical Production" being the most interesting. In
Dubious Battle is re-examined in one essay, "The Unity of
In Dubious Battle, " by Howard Levant, who relies on some
very close reading of the novel's imagery. But by far the

greatest number of essays, large and small amounting to
some forty items, have been devoted to The Grapes of Wrath.
It is worth noting that many of these essays concern themselves with some technical aspect of that novel, rather than
the ideological and sociological aspects pursued in the 1940's
and early 50's. Much of this criticism has continued, after
my own work and Shockley's essay, to explore the novel's
Biblical allusions and symbolism. Eric Carlson, in his
"Symbolism in The Grapes of Wrath," while admitting the
prevalence of the symbolism, denies both that it is "primary
to the structure of the novel" and that it gives that novel "an
essentially and thoroughly Christian meaning." In this argument he has been supported by Walter F. Taylor (of whom
more later), who insisted further that The Grapes of Wrath
"only hijacked part of the Christian story in order to turn
it to the illustrations of profoundly non-Christian meanings."
The battle was joined by several other essayists, for example H. Kelly Crockett, Charles T. Dougherty, Thomas
F. Dunn, Theodore Pollock, Gerard Cannon, Chris Browning, and Leonard Slade. Some brought more flexible inter-
pretations of the Bible to fit the words and actions of the
novel's characters. Others brought new parallels; for instance Tom as a Moses figure or even a St. Paul, or the
number of Joads corresponding to the disciples and the tribes
of Israel, etc.

Another aspect of the novel which has been seriously
attended to is its animal imagery. Through the work of
George Bluestone (Novel into Film) and Griffin and Freedman, criticism has moved from the mere repetition of Edmund Wilson's charge about Steinbeck's "animalism" to a
careful analysis of the symbolic meaning and thematic function of the animals and animal tropes in the novel. Bluestone was able to match the animal metaphors neatly to the
progression of the action; Griffin and Freedman in "Machines
and Animals: Pervasive Motifs in The Grapes of Wrath"
classified the animal tropes and categorized them according
to function. These three critics in fact demonstrated that
the novel cannot be understood without some such analysis.

Concerning the novel's themes there is the spectacle
of Walter Fuller Taylor in "The Grapes of Wrath Recon-
sidered" accusing that novel of "pernicious meanings"; those
of

hostility, bitterness, and contempt toward the middle classes, of antagonism toward religion in its

> organized forms, of the enjoyment of a Tobacco
> Road sort of slovenliness, of an easy going promis-
> cuity and animalism in sex, of Casy's curious
> transcendental mysticism [apparently on a par with
> the other vices]....

Mr. Taylor blames the critics' general failure to see these
"pernicious meanings" in the novel on "the amorphous state
of our general culture" and on the intellectuals' lack of
"clearly seen and firmly held values." Fortunately, such
a view of the novel, a throwback to the hysterics of some
reviewers thirty years ago, seems clearly silly now. In
contrast to this negativism there have been such affirmations
of the novel's enduring humanity as the essay by Pascal Covici, Jr., "Work and the Texture of The Grapes of Wrath";
the perceptive essay by John Reed, "The Grapes of Wrath
and the Esthetics of Indigence"; Betty Perez' "House and
Home: Thematic Symbols in The Grapes of Wrath"; and
perhaps my own "The Dynamics of Community in The Grapes
of Wrath," the latter appearing in From Irving to Steinbeck:
Studies in American Literature, Deakin and Lisca, eds. For
most readers today, as for Agnes Donohue, the novel seems
"richly symbolic, a mixture of myth and scripture." Thus
the journey motif becomes

> a complex symbol of fallen man's compulsive but
> doomed search for Paradise and ritual reenact-
> ment of the Fall. More than an historical, bib-
> lical, or sociological exodus, the journey of the
> Joads is a deeply mythical hegira of the hegira
> of the human spirit in a fallen world.

In addition to inspiring some of the best Steinbeck
criticism, The Grapes of Wrath has proved its viability in
other ways. There are Warren French's Companion, Donohue's Casebook collection of essays, various study guides,
and my own critical edition of the novel with various essays
for the Viking Press (in May of 1969, "in honor of John
Steinbeck and in commemoration of his greatest novel," a
conference of scholars was held at the University of Connecticut at which were read five papers on The Grapes of
Wrath, three of which--those by Pascal Covici, Jr. and
John Reed, mentioned above, and my own history of the novel's criticism--are reprinted in this Viking critical edition).

It would be unrealistic to expect each of Steinbeck's
novels to excite as much scholarly activity as has The

Grapes of Wrath, which is, after all, the peak of his achievement. But this activity will undoubtedly spread to other
works which still need perceptive analysis. That the basic
interest and raw energy for such activity does exist is evident from the success of the John Steinbeck Society (1966)
and the Steinbeck Quarterly (founded 1969), edited by Hayashi
with Robert DeMott as managing editor. Begun modestly as
a mimeographed Steinbeck Newsletter (1968) this quarterly is
now the central exchange for bibliography, scholarship, and
information. Its yearly monograph series, beginning with
Hayashi's John Steinbeck: A Guide to the Doctoral Dissertations (1946-1969) (1971), promises to become a valuable
contribution. There are other signs of this energy. Following the conference at Connecticut in 1969, Richard Astro, with the generous support of Oregon State University
and Ball State University (sponsor of the Steinbeck Quarterly), organized a two-day conference at Corvallis, Oregon in April of 1970, the proceedings of which have been
published in book form. Martha Cox, professor of English
at San Jose State College, procured that institution's support
for a three-day conference held on the campus in February
of 1971. The particular feature of this gathering was its focus on Steinbeck films. All of these conferences have been
successful in terms of the quality of scholarship displayed
and the interest generated.

Looking back from this present bustle of conferences
and scholarly publications to the lean Steinbeck years of
1950-1955, it is clear that the body of criticism is growing
rapidly. True, some of that growth has been mere fat, the
unscholarly repetition through ignorance of previously well-
developed ideas or, worse, the near-plagiarism of some who
must write although they have nothing new to say. But the
most recent work seems strong in muscle and bone, and
promises well for the future.

Notes

1. A portion of this essay appeared in The Wide World of
    John Steinbeck (New Brunswick, New Jersey: Rutgers
    University Press, 1958). The present essay is re-
    vised, amplified, and brought up to date.

2. The items referred to in the present essay are so nu-
    merous that in order to avoid excessive cluttering of
    the text I give only enough to enable the reader to

complete the reference for himself by consulting the
Hayashi bibliographies under the appropriate category.

3. For the convenience of some readers I have translated
all passages, but retained the original titles for reference.

2. STEINBECK SCHOLARSHIP:
RECENT TRENDS IN THE UNITED STATES

by Tetsumaro Hayashi

The literary reputation of John Steinbeck, the 1962 Nobel Prize winner, has begun to rise considerably, especially since his death in 1968. Such leading critics as Peter Lisca, Warren French, and Joseph Fontenrose have enlightened a number of Steinbeck students at home and abroad. Like Tedlock and Wicker's Steinbeck and His Critics (1957), Peter Lisca's The Wide World of John Steinbeck (1958) was instrumental in initiating this movement after World War II. The John Steinbeck Society, which was established in 1966, has been publishing the Steinbeck Quarterly since February, 1968 and recently initiated the Steinbeck Monograph Series (1970-). The journal, published under the joint-sponsorship of Ball State University and the John Steinbeck Society, has discovered promising scholars such as Richard Astro, John Ditsky (Canada), Reloy Garcia, Robert DeMott, and others. Since May, 1969 when the University of Connecticut sponsored the first Steinbeck Conference with the theme of The Grapes of Wrath and its impact on the 1930's, even further interest has been generated. Richard Astro, associate editor of the Steinbeck Quarterly, directed the 1970 Steinbeck Conference at Oregon State University. Both Astro and I edited the proceedings of the conference, Steinbeck: The Man and His Work, which was published by Oregon State University Press in April, 1971.

Martha H. Cox directed the 1971 Steinbeck Conference and Film Festival at San Jose State College with Peter Lisca as Consultant on March 26-28, 1971. Some of the papers presented there were published in the Steinbeck Quarterly (Special Conference Number, Summer, 1971) with Richard Astro as acting editor and Martha Cox as visiting associate editor.

The original Steinbeck Society was founded in 1966 by Preston Beyer (co-founder) and myself (founder) and grew to be a 53-member society by 1969. By September, 1971 it

listed more than 290 members in 13 nations (U. S. A. , Japan,
Canada, England, Australia, Germany, India, Korea, Malaysia,
Rumania, Switzerland, France, and Denmark) and 42 of the
United States. The Society sends its publications to 23
U. S. I. S. -sponsored libraries abroad and 13 Ball State Euro-
pean Centers. It is Ball State University that has made a
number of the Steinbeck Society-sponsored projects possible
since 1968.

The Society not only has such prominent Steinbeck
scholars and authors as Peter Lisca, Joseph Fontenrose,
and others as active members, but also has as contributing
members such noted Steinbeck collectors as Preston Beyer
of Columbus, Ohio, a business executive, and Roy S. Sim-
monds of England, a government official. It has Warren
French, one of the leading scholars in American literature,
the author and editor of several books on Steinbeck and related subjects, as president and senior advisor. Its members are from all walks of life: high school teachers, li-
brarians, book collectors, book sellers, poets, journalists,
lawyers, business executives, government officials, college
professors, students, housewives, and medical doctors. The
institutional memberships include most of the outstanding
university and public libraries at home and abroad.

As editor of the Steinbeck Quarterly and director of
the John Steinbeck Society, I am in a position to recognize
at least some of the significant directions in which Steinbeck critics seem to be currently moving. In my direct
contact with many of them I have observed the following
trends: (1) a conscious effort to treat more specific nar-
rower subjects in Steinbeck research, as Peter Lisca
pointed out at the Oregon State University Steinbeck Conference in 1970; (2) a growing interest in comparative studies between Steinbeck and other authors such as Faulkner,
Hemingway, and D. H. Lawrence; (3) an enthusiastic research on films and filmscripts based on Steinbeck's work[1];
(4) a steady effort to explore Steinbeck's minor works, including his short stories and articles originally published in
various magazines and newspapers; (5) an attempt to collect
Steinbeck's unpublished manuscripts and letters; (6) a serious interest in another comparative study between two works
such as a comparison between The Grapes of Wrath and In
Dubious Battle; Cannery Row and Sweet Thursday; and The
Winter of Our Discontent and America and Americans; (7)
projects to write biographies of Steinbeck; (8) a belated
critical interest in Ed Ricketts, Steinbeck's "artistic con-

science," whose influence upon Steinbeck has long been recognized but not yet fully assessed[2]; (9) a recent interest in
source studies of Steinbeck's fiction; (10) a serious interest
in "the Monterey Novels," as Warren French recently pointed
out, including especially Cannery Row and Sweet Thursday[3];
and finally (11) a special interest in Steinbeck's political
views, especially on the war in Viet Nam.[4]

Although Steinbeck has long suffered from both unkind
criticism and undeserved neglect from academic circles, his
reputation has been rising considerably in recent years. As
far as I know, at least ten doctoral dissertations are being
prepared at this moment in the United States alone and several more in India, Canada, Japan, England, France, and
Rumania. Serious scholars who are contributing to the
Steinbeck Quarterly, and other journals such as PMLA,
American Literature, Modern Fiction Studies, and Twentieth
Century Literature now have a sense of aesthetic distance,
an advantage which enables them to reassess more accurately Steinbeck's artistic triumphs and failures, his philosophy
of life, his image of man, and his contribution to American
literature.

The following book-length studies (chronologically arranged) including booklets and monographs may not only
serve as a basic guide to Steinbeck's major works in either
Viking, Bantam, or Random House editions, but also allow
Steinbeck students to glance at the history of Steinbeck criticism.

Lewis Gannet. John Steinbeck, Personal and Bibliographical Notes [booklet size]. New York: Viking Press,
1939 (reprinted by Folcroft; Pa.: Folcroft Press, 1970; a
brief but still valuable bibliographical source).
Harry T. Moore. The Novels of John Steinbeck: A
First Critical Study. Chicago: Normandie House, 1939 (reprinted by Port Washington, N.Y.: Kennikat Press, 1968;
the oldest book-length study but it still has a historical and
bibliographical value).
E. W. Tedlock, Jr. and C. V. Wicker (eds.). Steinbeck and His Critics: A Record of Twenty-Five Years.
Albuquerque: University of New Mexico Press, 1957 (reprinted in 1969 by the same press; a handy collection of articles by Warren French, Peter Lisca, Frederick I. Carpenter as well as Steinbeck's).
Peter Lisca. The Wide World of John Steinbeck. New
Brunswick, N.J.: Rutgers University Press, 1958 (reprinted

in 1961, 1965, and 1967 by the same press; the most definitive critical book; largely responsible for initiating the post-
war Steinbeck criticism in the United States; one of the most
frequently quoted books on Steinbeck).
    Warren French. John Steinbeck. New York: Twayne;
New Haven, Conn.: College and University Press, 1961 (an
extremely popular and enlightening book that has been translated into four foreign languages).
    F. W. Watt. John Steinbeck. New York: Grove
Press, 1962 (a popular introductory book; now out of print).
    Joseph Fontenrose. John Steinbeck: An Introduction
and Interpretation. New York: Barnes and Noble, 1963 (a
distinguished classical scholar's unique critical appraisal of
Steinbeck's major works).
    Warren French (ed.). A Companion to The Grapes of
Wrath. New York: Viking Press, 1963 (an excellent anthology of pertinent materials on the subject that gives the
reader a historical perspective on the reputation of this novelist; a handy reference book).
    Helmut Liedloff. Steinbeck in German Translational
Practices (Humanities Series, No. 1). Carbondale: Southern
Illinois University Press, 1965 [booklet length].
    Tetsumaro Hayashi. John Steinbeck: A Concise Bib-
liography (1930-1965). Introduction by Warren French.
Metuchen, N.J.: Scarecrow Press, 1967 (the only comprehensive bibliography available so far, although a revised,
enlarged, and selectively annotated edition is in preparation).
    Agnes McNeill Donohue (ed.). A Casebook on The
Grapes of Wrath. New York: Crowell, 1968 (a handy reference book, a collection of selected articles on the novel).
    Lester J. Marks. Thematic Design in the Novels of
John Steinbeck. The Hague, Netherlands: The Mouton Co.,
1969 (one of the most recent critical books; especially Chapters I and III are excellent).
    Richard O'Connor. John Steinbeck. New York: Mc-
Graw-Hill Co., 1970 (the only book-length biography availa-
ble so far; an interesting and sympathetic biography for
young people).
    John Clark Pratt. John Steinbeck. Grand Rapids,
Michigan: William B. Eerdmans, 1970 [booklet length]
(commendable bio-critical booklet).
    Richard Astro and Tetsumaro Hayashi (eds.). Stein-
beck: The Man and His Work: Proceedings of the 1970
Steinbeck Conference. Corvallis: Oregon State University
Press, 1971 (essay by Robert DeMott, Charles Metzger,
John Ditsky, Peter Lisca, and others on Cannery Row,
Sweet Thursday, Viva Zapata!, etc.).

James Gray. <u>John Steinbeck</u> (University of Minnesota
Pamphlets on American Writers, No. 94). Minneapolis:
University of Minnesota Press, 1971 [booklet length] (a brief
survey of Steinbeck as a novelist).
Tetsumaro Hayashi (ed.). <u>John Steinbeck: A Guide
to the Doctoral Dissertations (1946-1969)</u> (Steinbeck Monograph Series, No. 1). Muncie, Indiana: Ball State University, 1971 [booklet length] (a collection of 16 dissertation
abstracts with Hayashi's article, "Recent Steinbeck Criticism
in the United States").

In preparation:

1. Richard Astro. <u>Steinbeck and Ed Ricketts</u> [book-
let length] (Steinbeck Monograph Series, No. 3).
2. Reloy Garcia. <u>Steinbeck and D. H. Lawrence</u>
[booklet length] (Steinbeck Monograph Series, No. 2).
3. Tetsumaro Hayashi and Robert DeMott (eds.).
<u>Steinbeck in Perspective.</u>
4. Tetsumaro Hayashi. <u>Steinbeck Criticism (1930-
1971)</u>.
5. Peter Lisca. <u>The Grapes of Wrath: Text and
Criticism.</u>
6. Peter Lisca. <u>John Steinbeck: Myth and Biology.</u>

To conclude, these Steinbeck critics who are members
of the John Steinbeck Society are active with the following
purpose in mind: "to add new dimensions to our understanding of John Steinbeck by encouraging the study of the distinction between these two Steinbecks (the involved journalist and
the detached artist) and reaffirming in the two distinct areas
of American cultural studies and fictional aesthetics the
separate, yet ultimately related importance of both. "5

                              Notes

1. On February 26-28, 1970, San Jose State College sponsored the Steinbeck Film Festival with Martha Cox
   as director and Peter Lisca as consultant. In addition, Professor Lisca, who helped Mr. Don Wrye do
   a short film on Steinbeck for the U. S. I. S. , is com-
   pleting a film for Lee Mendelson Productions to be
   called "Forty Years of American Life as Seen in the
   Works of John Steinbeck, " which will be a television

special.

2. Richard Astro has been working on the subject and his
   monograph on Steinbeck and Ed Ricketts will be published by Ball State University in 1974.

3. Robert DeMott, "Steinbeck and the Creative Process:
   First Manifesto to End the Bringdown against Sweet
   Thursday" in SMHW, pp. 157-178.
   Richard Astro, "Steinbeck's Bittersweet Thursday," SQ,
   4 (Spring, 1971), 36-48.
   Robert M. Benton, "The Ecological Nature of Cannery
   Row" in SMHW, pp. 131-139.

4. Andreas Poulakidas, "Steinbeck, Kazantzakis, and Social-
   ism," SQ, 3 (Summer, 1970), 62-72.
   George H. Spies, III, "John Steinbeck's In Dubious Bat-
   tle and Robert Penn Warren's Night Rider," SQ, 4
   (Spring, 1971), 48-55.
   Harland E. Nelson, "Steinbeck's Politics Then and Now,"
   Antioch Review, 27 (Spring, 1967), 118-133.
   Sanford E. Marovitz, "John Steinbeck and Adlai Steven-
   son," SQ, 3 (Summer, 1970), 51-62.
   Warren French, "John Steinbeck's Politics: The An-
   achronism" in The Politics of Nobility ed. by George
   A. Panichas (New York: Hawthorn Books, 1971),
   pp. 196-306.

3. A SELECTED BIBLIOGRAPHY

by Tetsumaro Hayashi

I. Doctoral Dissertations (1946-1969)

The reputation of the late John Steinbeck, the 1962 Nobel Prize winner, one of the important American novelists in the twentieth century, has steadily risen since his death in 1968. One of the substantial proofs of his steady appeal to the public is reflected in the fact that since 1946 seventeen Ph. D. dissertations and one doctor of education dissertation have been written about him in English, and that the dissertations of Peter Lisca and Lester J. Marks have been published as books, respectively in 1958 and 1969. These English-language dissertations were prepared by sixteen Americans, one Canadian, and one Indian in the following frequency: 1946 (one dissertation), 1953 (1), 1955 (1), 1957 (1), 1961 (2), 1962 (1), 1963 (1), 1965 (1), 1966 (3), 1967 (2), 1968 (2), and 1969 (2).

Their subjects vary greatly. In fact the eighteen dissertations deal with eighteen diversified aspects of Steinbeck: (1) the artistic development (Lisca, 1955); (2) the biological naturalism (Taylor, 1961); (3) the college freshman's response to The Grapes of Wrath (Wilson, 1963); (4) Steinbeck's depression novels (Feied, 1968); (5) the element of compassion (Satyanarayana of India, 1968); (6) a cultural analysis of Travels with Charley in Search of America (Johnson, 1966); (7) the human emotion and early fiction (Casimir, 1966); (8) the land-nostalgia (Ditsky, 1967); (9) the longer fiction (Levant, 1962); (10) the moral world (Ogulnik of Canada, 1953); (11) the primitivism and pastoral form in early fiction (Alexander, 1965); (12) the use of psychology (Freel, 1946); (13) the reputation since World War II (Smith, 1967); (14) the setting and animal tropes (Bleeker, 1969); (15) the symbolic family (Wallis, 1966); (16) the thematic continuity (Marks, 1961); (17) the vision of nature and ideal man (Astro, 1969); and (18) the young characters (Young, 1957).

174

These doctoral dissertations on diversified aspects of Steinbeck were accepted by fifteen universities in the United States, Canada, and India; that is, Columbia University (one dissertation) Cornell University (1), Louisiana State University (1), New York University (2), Osmania University, India (1), Stanford University (1), Syracuse University (1), the University of California, Berkeley (1), the University of Kansas (1), the University of Michigan (1), the University of Montreal (1), the University of Nebraska (1), the University of New Mexico (1), the University of Texas (2), the University of Washington (1), and the University of Wisconsin (1).

The following checklist, chronologically arranged, records all known doctoral dissertations written in English between 1946 and 1969. Although I might have failed to record some, I trust this list will serve Steinbeck students as a springboard for further original studies.

1. Freel, Eugene L. "Comparative Study Between Certain Concepts and Principles of Modern Psychology and the Main Writings of John Steinbeck, " New York University, 1946.
2. Ogulnik, Maurice A. "The Moral World of Steinbeck, " University of Montreal, Canada, 1953.
3. Lisca, Peter. "The Art of John Steinbeck: An Analysis and Interpretation of Its Development, " University of Wisconsin, 1955.
4. Young, Leo Vernon. "Values of the Young Characters in the Fiction of Dos Passos, Hemingway, and Steinbeck, " Stanford University, 1957.
5. Marks, Lester Jay. "A Study of Thematic Continuity in the Novels of John Steinbeck, " Syracuse University, 1961.
6. Taylor, Horace Platt, Jr. "The Biological Naturalism of John Steinbeck, " Louisiana State University, 1961.
7. Levant, Howard Stanley. "A Critical Study of the Longer Fiction of John Steinbeck, " Cornell University, 1962.
8. Wilson, James Robert. "Responses of College Freshmen to Three Novels (J. D. Salinger's The Catcher in the Rye, John Steinbeck's The Grapes of Wrath, and E. Hemingway's A Farewell to Arms), University of California, Berkeley, 1963 (Doctor of Education dissertation).
9. Alexander, Stanley Gerald. "Primitivism and Pastoral Form in John Steinbeck's Early Fiction, " University of Texas, 1965.

        10. Casimir, Louis J., Jr. "Human Emotion and
the Early Novels of John Steinbeck," University of Texas,
1966.
        11. Johnson, Charles Daniel. "A Pedagogical Study
in Contrastive Cultural Analysis Illustrated by Steinbeck's
Travels with Charley in Search of America," University of
Michigan, 1966.
        12. Wallis, Prentiss Bascom, Jr. "John Steinbeck:
The Symbolic Family," University of Kansas, 1966.
        13. Ditsky, John Michael. "Land-Nostalgia in the
Novels of Faulkner, Cather, and Steinbeck," New York University, 1967.
        14. Smith, Donald Boone. "The Decline in John
Steinbeck's Critical Reputation since World War II," University of New Mexico, 1967.
        15. Satyanarayana, M. R. "The Element of Com-
passion in the World of John Steinbeck," Osmania University,
India, 1968.
        16. Feied, Frederick. "Steinbeck's Depression Nov-
els: The Ecological Basis," Columbia University, 1968.
        17. Astro, Richard. "Into the Cornucopia: Stein-
beck's Vision of Nature and the Ideal Man," University of
Washington, 1969.
        18. Bleeker, Gary. "Setting and Animal Tropes in
the Fiction of John Steinbeck," University of Nebraska, 1969.

II. Articles Since 1965

Aaron, Daniel. "The Radical Humanism of John Steinbeck:
     The Grapes of Wrath Thirty Years Later," Saturday
     Review, 51 (September 28, 1968), 26-27; 55-56.
Adrian, Daryl. "Steinbeck's New Image of America and the
     Americans," Steinbeck Quarterly, 3 (1970), 83-92.
Alexander, Stanley. "Cannery Row: Steinbeck's Pastoral
     Poem," Western American Literature, 2 (1968), 281-95.
Alexander, Stanley. "The Conflict of Form in Tortilla Flat,"
     American Literature, 40 (1968), 58-66.
Anderson, Hilton. "Steinbeck's 'Flight,'" Explicator, 38
     (1969), Item 12.
Astro, Richard. "Steinbeck and Mainwaring: Two Californ-
     ians for the Earth," Steinbeck Quarterly, 3 (1970), 3-11.
Astro, Richard. "Steinbeck's Post-War Trilogy: A Return
     to Nature and the Natural Man," Twentieth Century Lit-
     erature, 16 (1970), 109-122.
Beyer, Preston. "Collecting John Steinbeckiana," Steinbeck
     Quarterly, 2 (1969), 56-59.
Bode, Elroy. "The World on Its Own Terms: A Brief for

Steinbeck, Miller and Simenon," Southwest Review, 53 (1968), 406-416.

Brown, D. Russell. "The Natural Man in John Steinbeck's Non-Teleological Tales," Ball State University Forum, 7 (Spring 1966), 47-59.

Browning, Chris. "Grape Symbolism in The Grapes of Wrath," Discourse, 11 (1968), 129-140.

Collier, Peter. "The Winter of John Steinbeck," Ramparts, 6 (July 1967), 59-61.

Covici, Pascal, Jr. "In Memoriam: John Steinbeck," Steinbeck Newsletter, 2 (1969), 18.

Crockett, H. Kelly. "The Other Cheek," College English, 24 (April 1963), 567.

Ditsky, John. "From Oxford to Salinas: Comparing Faulkner and Steinbeck," Steinbeck Quarterly, 2 (1969), 51-55.

Ditsky, John M. "Music from a Dark Cave: Organic Form in Steinbeck's Fiction," The Journal of Narrative Technique, 1 (1971), 59-67.

Dvorak, Wilfred Paul. "Notes Towards the Education of the Heart," Iowa English Year Book, 10 (1965), 46-49.

Fontenrose, Joseph. "Memorial Statement on John Steinbeck," Steinbeck Newsletter, 2 (1969), 19-20.

French, Warren. "Message: John Steinbeck (February 27, 1902 to December 20, 1968)," Steinbeck Newsletter, 2 (1969), 3-9.

Frietzsche, Arthur H. "Steinbeck as a Western Author," Proceedings of the Utah Academy of Sciences, Arts, and Letters, 42 (1965), 11-13.

Galbraith, John Kenneth. "John Steinbeck: Footnote for a Memoir," Atlantic, 224 (1969), 65-67.

Goldsmith, Arnold L. "Thematic Rhythm in The Red Pony," College English, 26 (February 1965), 391-394.

Golemba, Henry L. "Steinbeck's Attempt to Escape the Literary Fallacy," Modern Fiction Studies, 15 (1969), 231-239.

Gordon, Ernest. "The Winter of Our Discontent," Princeton Seminary Bulletin, 15 (1962), 44-47.

Griffin, Robert J. and Freedman, William A. "Machines and Animals: Pervasive Motifs in The Grapes of Wrath," Journal of English and Germanic Philology, 62 (1963), 569-580.

Hashiguchi, Yasuo. "Japanese Translations of Steinbeck's Works (1939-69)," Steinbeck Quarterly, 3 (1970), 93-106.

Hauck, Richard B. "The Comic Christ and the Modern Reader," College English 31 (1970), 498-506 [Jim Casy in The Grapes of Wrath; Faulkner, and others].

Steinbeck's Literary Dimension

Houghton, Donald E. "'Westering' in 'The Leader of the
  People'," Western American Literature, 4 (1969), 117-
  124.
Jackson, Frank H. "Economics in Literature (The Grapes
  of Wrath)," Duquesne Review, 3 (Spring 1958), 80-85.
Jones, Lawrence William. "A Little Play in Your Head:
  Parable Form in John Steinbeck's Post-War Fiction,"
  Genre, 3 (1970), 55-63.
Jones, Lawrence W. "A Novel on Steinbeck's Earliest
  Stories," Steinbeck Quarterly, 2 (1969), 59-60.
Jones, Lawrence William. "Personal History," Saturday
  Review, 52 (December 20, 1969), 25-26.
Jones, Lawrence William. "Random Thoughts from Paris:
  Steinbeck's Un Américain à New York et à Paris,"
  Steinbeck Quarterly, 3 (1970), 27-30.
Jones, Lawrence William. "The Real Authorship of Stein-
  beck's 'Verse'," Steinbeck Quarterly, 3 (1970), 11-12.
Jones, Lawrence William. "An Uncited Post-War Steinbeck
  Story: 'The Short Short Story of Mankind'," Steinbeck
  Quarterly, 3 (1970), 30-31.
Kingsbury, Stewart A. "Steinbeck's Use of Dialect and Ar-
  chaic Language," Steinbeck Newsletter, 2 (1969), 28-33.
Levant, Howard. "Tortilla Flat: The Shape of John Stein-
  beck's Career," PMLA, 85 (1970), 1087-1095.
Lisca, Peter. "In Memory of John Steinbeck" [a poem],
  Steinbeck Newsletter, 2 (1969), 20-21.
Lisca, Peter. "Steinbeck and Hemingway," Steinbeck News-
  letter, 2 (1969), 9-17.
McCarthy, Paul. "House and Shelter as Symbol in The
  Grapes of Wrath," South Dakota Review, 5 (Winter
  1967-68), 48-67.
McMahan, Elizabeth E. "'The Chrysanthemums': Study of
  a Woman's Sexuality," Modern Fiction Studies, 14 (1968),
  453-458.
Madison, C. A. "Covici: Steinbeck's Editor, Collaborator,
  and Conscience," Saturday Review, 49 (June 25, 1966),
  15-16.
Madison, Charles A. "The Friendship of Covici and Stein-
  beck," Chicago Jewish Forum, 24 (Summer 1966), 293-
  296.
Mandelbaum, Bernard. "John Steinbeck's 'The Snake': The
  Structure of a Dream," English Record, 26 (1966), 24-
  26.
Marks, Lester J. "John Ernst Steinbeck: 1902-1968,"
  Steinbeck Newsletter, 2 (1969), 21-22.
Marovitz, Sanford E. "John Steinbeck and Adlai Stevenson,"
  Steinbeck Quarterly, 3 (1970), 51-62.

Moore, Harry T. "John Steinbeck: A Memorial Statement,"
 Steinbeck Newsletter, 2 (1969), 23.
Moore, William L. "In Memoriam," Steinbeck Newsletter,
 2 (1969), 24.
Morsberger, Robert E. "In Defense of 'Westering'," West-
 ern American Literature, 5 (Summer 1970), 143-146.
 (On "The Leader of the People" in The Long Valley).
Nagle, J. M. "View of Literature Too Often Neglected:
 The Pearl," English Journal, 58 (1969), 399-407.
Nelson, Harlan S. "Steinbeck's Politics Then and Now,"
 Antioch Review, 27 (1967), 118-133.
Nichols, Lewis. "The Writers in the Sand," New York
 Times Book Review, August 4, 1968. Section 7, pp.
 8, 10.
Nossen, Evon. "The Beast-Man Theme in the Works of
 John Steinbeck," Ball State University Forum, 7 (Spring
 1966), 52-64.
Osborne, William R. "The Texts of Steinbeck's 'The Chrysan-
 themums'," Modern Fiction Studies, 12 (Winter 1966-67),
 479-484.
Poulakidas, Andreas K. "Steinbeck, Kazantzakis, and So-
 cialism," Steinbeck Quarterly, 3 (1970), 62-72.
Robles, M. "Cain--An Unfortunate?" Modern Language
 (London), 50 (1969), 57-59 [Cain in Unamuno, Baudelaire,
 Beckett, and Steinbeck].
Roland, Bartel. "Proportioning in Fiction: The Pearl and
 Silas Marner," English Journal, 56 (April 1967), 542-
 546.
Scoville, Samuel. "The Weltanschauung of Steinbeck and
 Hemingway: An Analysis of Themes," English Journal,
 56 (1967), 60-63. (The Pearl and The Old Man and the
 Sea).
Shaw, P. "Steinbeck: The Shape of a Career," Saturday
 Review, 52 (February 8, 1969), 10-14.
Slade, Leonard A., Jr. "The Use of Biblical Allusions in
 The Grapes of Wrath," College Language Associate
 Journal, 11 (1968), 241-247.
Taylor, Horace P., Jr. "John Steinbeck--The Quest," Mc-
 Neese Review, 10 (1965), 33-45.
Tedlock, E. W., Jr. "A Pathos and a Power," (Memorial
 Statement), Steinbeck Newsletter, 2 (1969), 27-28.
Vogel, Dan. "Steinbeck's 'Flight': The Myth of Manhood,"
 Fiction: Form and Experience by William W. Jones.
 Lexington, Mass.: Heath, 1969, pp. 376-378.
Wyatt, Bryant N. "Experimentation as Technique: The Pro-
 test Novels of John Steinbeck," Discourse, 12 (1969),
 143-153.

CONTRIBUTORS

ASTRO, RICHARD. Associate professor of English, Oregon State University; associate editor of the Steinbeck Quarterly; director of the Oregon State University-sponsored Steinbeck Conference, 1970; co-editor of a book, Steinbeck: The Man and His Work with Tetsumaro Hayashi (1971); published on Fitzgerald, Norris, and Steinbeck in such journals as Modern Fiction Studies, Steinbeck Quarterly, Twentieth Century Literature, Western American Literature; Ph. D. (University of Washington).

DITSKY, JOHN. Associate professor of English, University of Windsor, Windsor, Canada; poetry editor of the Windsor Review; discussion leader of the MLA Steinbeck Seminar, 1972; author of articles, plays, and short stories; contributing editor of the Steinbeck Quarterly; a poet who has published poems in over fifty journals in the U. S. A. and Canada; Ph. D. (New York University).

FRENCH, WARREN. Professor of English and chairman of the Department of English, IUPU at Indianapolis; president of the John Steinbeck Society of America; senior editorial advisor of the Steinbeck Quarterly; author and/ or editor of numerous books on Steinbeck and other subjects including John Steinbeck (1961), and A Companion to The Grapes of Wrath (1963); published widely in such journals as American Literature, American Quarterly, and Western Humanities Review; Ph. D. (University of Texas).

GRIBBEN, JOHN. Associate professor of English, Kent State University; visiting professor, Graduate Theological Seminary, Antioch College, Ohio; Ph. D. (University of Colorado).

HAYASHI, TETSUMARO. Naturalized U. S. citizen; founder and director of the John Steinbeck Society of America (1966-); founder and editor of the Steinbeck Quarterly (1968-); founder and general editor of the Steinbeck Monograph Series (1970-); associate professor of

English and member of Doctoral Faculty at Ball State
University (1968-), where he is currently directing
three Steinbeck dissertations; a specialist on Robert
Greene and Shakespeare; a Rotary International Junior
Scholar, 1955-56; a Folger Senior Fellow, 1972; author
and/or editor of eight books and three monographs including John Steinbeck: A Concise Bibliography (1930-
1965) with an introduction by Warren French (Scarecrow Press, 1967), Steinbeck: The Man and His Work
ed. with Richard Astro (Oregon State University
Press, 1971), and John Steinbeck: A Guide to the Doctoral Dissertations (1946-1969) (Muncie, Indiana: Ball
State University, 1971); published more than 40 articles on Robert Greene, Ben Jonson, Shakespeare,
Steinbeck, etc. in U. S. A. , Japan, and India and twelve
short stories in the United States; Ph. D. (Kent State
University).

†JONES, LAWRENCE WILLIAM. Former professor of English, Algonquin College of Applied Arts and Technology,
Ottawa, Canada; published on Steinbeck in Canadian Literature, Genre, Saturday Review, Religion in Life,
Serif, and Steinbeck Quarterly; died in an automobile
accident in England, January 1, 1971, when he was research tutor in American studies at the University of
Leicester, England; regarded as one of the promising
young Steinbeck scholars; M. A. (Carleton University,
Canada).

LISCA, PETER. Professor of English, University of Flori-
da; author of The Wide World of John Steinbeck (1958).
published widely on Chaucer, Fitzgerald, Hemingway,
and Steinbeck in leading journals; Smith-Mundt Lecturer
in American Literature, University of Zaragosa, Spain
in 1958-59; editor of the Viking critical edition of The
Grapes of Wrath; co-editor of From Irving to Steinbeck;
contributor to several volumes of Steinbeck criticism;
Ph. D. (University of Wisconsin).

MAROVITZ, SANFORD E. Associate professor of English,
Kent State University; Fulbright Lecturer of English,
University of Athens, 1965-67; published articles in such
journals as American Literary Realism, American Quarterly, Modern Fiction Studies, Philological Quarterly,
and Steinbeck Quarterly; Ph. D. (Duke University).

PETERSON, RICHARD F. Assistant professor of English

and director of the Basic English Studies, Southern Illinois University; published articles on Faulkner, Joyce, D. H. Lawrence, and Steinbeck; Ph. D. (Kent State University).

POULAKIDAS, ANDREAS K. Associate professor of English and comparative literature, Ball State University; published on Nikos Kazantzakis in Comparative Literature, Comparative Studies, Journal of Modern Literature, Philological Quarterly, Southern Humanities Review, and Steinbeck Quarterly; Ph. D. (Indiana University).

SIEFKER, DONALD L. (indexer) Executive editor and library coordinator of the Steinbeck Quarterly; head of the Division of Information Sources and Reference, and Instructor of Library Service, Ball State University; published in the Steinbeck Quarterly; associate compiler of An Annotated Checklist of the BSU Special Steinbeck Collection (forthcoming) with Tetsumaro Hayashi (1972). M. A. (Indiana University).

SPIES, GEORGE H., III. President of Lambda Iota Tau and doctoral candidate in English, Ball State University; preparing a dissertation on Steinbeck under the direction of Professor Tetsumaro Hayashi; published articles and book reviews in Steinbeck Quarterly; M. A. (Ball State University).

STEELE, JOAN. Lecturer of English and program coordinator and academic consultant for "Insight: Human Values in Urban Living," a pilot program in adult education, University of California at Los Angeles; published in Bulletin of Bibliography and Steinbeck Quarterly; Ph. D. (UCLA).

INDEX

183

DATE DUE

MAR 9 '83	APR 6 '88	
JUN 7 '83	APR 22 '88	
NOV 9 '83	APR 23 '90	
NOV 13 '84		
NOV 27 '84	MAY 09 '90	
DEC 14 '84	MAY 17	
FEB 7 '85	26	
APR 11 '85	NOV 26 '91	
JUN 31 '85	DEC 14 1993	
JUL 15 '85		
JUL 29 '85	JAN 28 1994	
AUG 9 '85	MAR 1 5 1996	
OCT 8 '85	MAR 0 3 1998	
NOV 30 '85	MAR 0 2 1999	
	MAR 0 2 1999	
APR 4 '86		
APR 18 '86		
JUN 3 '86		
JUN 17 '86		
GAYLORD		PRINTED IN U.S.A.